THE ANGLER WHO LANDED A PRIZE CATCH!

There was a knock at the surgery door. Before I'd time to say 'Come in', in walked a big man, wearing a tweed hat, anorak, and tweed trousers tucked into a pair of wellington boots. He walked stiffly, with his right hand clutched to the corresponding buttock.

'I'll have to shake hands with me left, doctor,' he said as I greeted him.

'Fine by me,' I said. 'Won't you sit down?'

'If it's all the same to you,' he said, wincing slightly, 'I'd rather stand.'

It was John Denton, River Authority head bailiff on the Tadchester end of the River Tad.

He turned around and lifted his anorak. There, dangling from the seat of his pants, was a large piece of pink metal. 'It's a Devon minnow,' said John - a salmon lure. It was dangling from a vicious triangular hook which had obviously gone in much further than the tweed.

D0716618

Also by Robert Clifford in Sphere Books:

JUST HERE, DOCTOR
LOOK OUT, DOCTOR!
OH DEAR, DOCTOR!
WHAT NEXT, DOCTOR?

Not There, Doctor
DR ROBERT CLIFFORD

Illustrated by Nick Baker

SPHERE BOOKS LIMITED
London and Sydney

First published in Great Britain by
Pelham Books Ltd 1978
Copyright © Robert D. Clifford 1978
Published by Sphere Books Ltd 1980
30–32 Gray's Inn Road, London WC1X 8JL
Reprinted 1981 (twice), 1984

TRADE
MARK

This book is sold subject to the condition that
it shall not, by way of trade or otherwise, be lent,
re-sold, hired out or otherwise circulated without
the publisher's prior consent in any form of
binding or cover other than that in which it is
published and without a similar condition
including this condition being imposed on the
subsequent purchaser

Set in Monotype Baskerville

Printed and bound in Great Britain by
Collins, Glasgow

For MURIEL GOAMAN

who started me putting pen to paper

Prologue

Life is a tragedy, for we are all born eventually to die. We survive our tragedies by laughing at them.

'*A friend once told me that when he was under the influence of ether he dreamed he was turning over the pages of a great book, in which he knew he would find, on the last page, the meaning of life.*

'*The pages of the book were alternately tragic and comic, and he turned page after page, his excitement growing, not only because he was approaching the answer, but because he couldn't know, until he arrived, on which side of the book the final page would be. At last it came: the universe opened up to him in a hundred words: and they were uproariously funny.*

'*He came back to consciousness crying with laughter, remembering everything. He opened his lips to speak. It was then that the great and comic answer plunged back out of his reach.*'

CHAPTER 1

The voice on the telephone left no doubt about the urgency of the call.

'Come straight away, doctor. It's our Mary. She's bleeding to death.'

The phone was abruptly replaced. It was eleven o'clock at night. Mary? Mary who?

There was one clue: I thought I recognised the voice as that of Mrs Prentice. She had an eighteen-year-old daughter Mary, and I knew where they lived – 5 Salterns Terrace, Up-the-Hill. But the message had given no clue to where 'our Mary' was bleeding from, or why.

I grabbed my medical case, jumped in my car, and

headed off as fast as I could for Salterns Terrace, hoping at least that my diagnosis of the name and address was correct.

It was. Number 5 Salterns Terrace was ablaze with lights. The voice of a young girl, presumably Mary, could be heard screaming right down the street. I rushed in the open front door, pushed my way through a group of peering neighbours, and found Mary – very much alive and screaming at the top of her voice. Her mother and father stood at either side of her with blood-soaked towels pressed to her ears.

I saw immediately what the trouble was, and knew that Mary was going to be all right . . .

When I was a hospital resident, each particular post I took became after a few weeks the one I was definitely going to specialise in. When I was a house surgeon, I was going to become a surgeon; when I was a house physician, I was going to be a physician; when I was doing midwifery and obstetrics, gynaecology was going to be my speciality. There was only one exception. I did a four-week locum in psychiatry, and resolved soon and firmly never to be a psychiatrist.

Later, in general practice, I was still able to pursue some of my skills in medicine and obstetrics but through sheer lack of practice my surgical skills slowly dwindled. I clung on obstinately as long as I could to the few surgical procedures I was still allowed to do. One of these was the removal of sebaceous cysts – lumps, mainly on the scalp, which could be surgically removed under local anaesthetic.

My operating sessions were conducted after-hours in the surgery. Sebaceous cyst surgery tended to be rather messy, with lots of blood, and Gladys, our senior receptionist, scowled her disapproval whenever I took time out to do some. Eventually one of my partners – Henry Johnson, FRCS, who was the surgeon at the local hospital – with support from Gladys, persuaded me that it was much better if *he* did this minor surgery in the Casualty Department of the hospital.

'It's much cleaner if I do it there,' said Henry, 'it doesn't keep our surgery staff late, and,' he added, with a twinkle in his eye, 'I *am* rather better at it than you are.'

Reluctantly I succumbed to the pressure. It left me with only one outlet for my surgical skills – ear piercing.

I became very proficient at this art, was even thought to be better than the Tadchester jeweller. I attracted more customers than he did, not just for my skill but because I was a National Health Service doctor and could not charge my patients for this service, whereas the Tadchester jeweller charged them £1.

Mary Prentice, a sweet eighteen-year-old, came timidly to have her ears pierced. She was nervous and apprehensive. Happily, everything went like clockwork. Sometimes one fumbles trying to get the gold sleepers into the pierced holes. My technique was old-fashioned but reliable. A dot with my pen on the earlobe as a target, a cork behind the ear, a quick spray of freezing solution and a large hollow hypodermic needle plunged straight through the lobe into the cork. The end of the sleeper was stuck into the open end of the hypodermic needle when I had disengaged it from the cork. The operation was then completed by pulling the needle back through the earlobe, bringing the sleeper end with it.

Mary had rather fancy sleepers, each with a little star on it, which I admired. They gave her a gypsy-like look, and certainly suited her.

. . . so when I arrived at 5 Salterns Terrace, diagnosis was instant and easy; removing the towels from Mary's ears confirmed it.

Mary had rushed home to change a jumper. As she pulled the jumper over her head, it had caught in the little star shapes on her sleepers – and torn the sleepers right through both earlobes. Poor Mary!

I dressed her wounds and drove her to the hospital

3

where Henry carefully stitched up her torn lobes.

It was a great lesson to me. From then on I warned everyone whose ears I pierced of how easily this could happen. But it was not a lesson to Mary. One year later she turned up again in my surgery, earlobes completely healed and with not a sign of a scar. 'Would you mind piercing my ears again, doctor?' she said, blushing.

'Certainly, Mary,' I said, 'providing, in future, you keep any stars in your eyes and not on your earrings.'

I was the junior partner in a group of four in a little Somerset town called Tadchester. Tadchester (population 6500) stands on the estuary of the River Tad, in one of the most beautiful parts of the Somerset coast. It is a market town, with some fishing, some light industry, and a great deal of farming. Six miles north is Thudrock Colliery, half of whose work force lives in Tadchester.

The town is split in two by the River Tad, and further split by the large hill which dominates one side of the river. The other side of the river is flat pastureland, stretching off to marshes and the sea coast. You are not just a Tadchester resident – you are strictly Up-the-Hill or Down-the-Hill. It has important social distinctions as whereas the population Down-the-Hill tend to be made up of Haves, the population Up-the-Hill tend to be the Have-nots.

We were the only general practice in the town, and in addition to our general practice duties we took care of the local hospital. The four partners each had a special interest at the hospital: Steve Maxwell, the senior partner, had a special interest in medicine; Henry Johnson, the second senior and sebaceous cyst poacher, was the surgeon; Jack Hart, the third partner, was the anaesthetist; and I, as the junior dogsbody, did most of the running around and was reckoned to be the expert in midwifery.

We practised from a central surgery Down-the-Hill, above which I had a bachelor flat and fended mostly for

4

myself, scrambled eggs and baked beans playing the main role in most of my menus.

I had been in Tadchester for two years and had recently become engaged: in fact, I had been back home from London for only five hours when I was called to Mary's bleeding ears. I had got engaged in London on New Year's Eve, two days before I returned, so had yet to announce my news in Tadchester, and I wondered what sort of reaction it might bring.

I had reached a horrific situation the previous summer when three of the local availables – Marjorie de Wyrebock of the riding school; Gwendoline Jacobs, the local beauty queen; and Brenda Collins, an old flame – had all tried to stake their claims on me in the same evening at the Tadchester Carnival Ball. I escaped by fleeing on holiday, with my mother as chaperone and bodyguard. While on holiday, I met Pamela, to whom I became engaged at my old London hospital's New Year Ball.

My first surgery to be held in the New Year was the morning after the torn earlobes episode. I wondered when would be the best time to announce my engagement. I would tell my partners when we met for morning coffee, but how and when to tell the surgery staff – not least the town – I still had not decided.

I didn't have to make a decision. I was embraced by Gladys, our senior receptionist, as soon as I came through the surgery door. 'Congratulations, Dr Bob,' she said, 'and not before time.'

Mary and Jill, our dispenser and junior receptionist, came up and kissed me, and offered their congratulations.

Tadchester had not let me down.

Somehow, as happens in most small communities, everyone seemed to know what you were going to do before you knew it yourself. As one of the local councillors once told me – 'It is not we councillors who break the secrets of

5

the confidential meetings – it's those we tell in confidence afterwards who let us down.'

I had been eased out of the difficulty of announcing my engagement, but still had the problem of my three original lady suitors. Pam, my wife-to-be, lived in Surrey, well away from the practice. My courting had all taken place out of Tadchester; Pam had visited the town only twice, briefly, and had therefore not registered on the community's sense of proprietorship as my possible future wife.

I started to go through the pile of mail that had accumulated on my desk while I had been away. One scented envelope. Help! I opened it anxiously. It was from Gwendoline Jacobs. Dear Gwendoline. Childlike, direct, tantalisingly over-developed and hopelessly over-sexed.

'Dear Dr Bob,' it read. 'Just a note to say I have been given a job in the Piccadilly Strip Bar. Do look me up if you are in London. I can always give you a bed for the night.'

It was written in a large, childish hand, and the bottom of the page was covered in large kisses. Gwendoline's openness always made me smile. I felt that in a strip bar she would at last come into her own.

Amongst the pile of hospital reports and letters there was a note from Brenda Collins. Brenda was a London midwife with whom, in our student days, I had had a long and idyllic affair. Things had changed after I qualified and Brenda went off to do her midwifery. She developed a taste for bright lights and monied specialists and became engaged to an obstetrician bound for Harley Street, but the engagement didn't work out. That was why Brenda turned up on that disastrous Carnival evening to press her claim on me. My last vision was of her standing there, horrified, after I had been sick all down the front of her sequinned dress.

The note was brief. 'Dear Bob,' she wrote. 'In the time we have been apart you seem to have turned into a

6

drunken degenerate. I do not wish to have anything more to do with you.'

There was one letter – or rather, card – that made my heart sink. It was brief and to the point. 'Commander and Mrs de Wyrebock request your company for cocktails on Sunday, 12th January, at 12 noon.'

I felt the card should have read, 'Mrs and Commander de Wyrebock command your company for cocktails . . .' There was no doubt that Mrs de Wyrebock was much more the commander than her husband. She never requested anybody to do anything: she just ordered them to report.

On my last visit to the de Wyrebocks, because of a small misunderstanding in the vinery I had virtually been chased from the house. The Commander seemed to have thought that my intentions towards his daughter were not entirely honourable. But my last meeting with horse-mad Marjorie at the fated Carnival Ball had left me in no doubt that she had picked me out as a desirable mount.

Two down, and one to go.

I couldn't believe that Marjorie would be as easily got rid of as my other two suitors. She was older, had begun to reach the desperate stage, and was severely handicapped in the marital stakes by two rows of teeth which would have looked good on a horse but which didn't do much for her.

There was no way that I could cross this bridge before I came to it, so I got down to my first surgery after the winter break.

It was packed. The news of my engagement apparently was not just confined to my surgery staff; the whole of the town appeared to know. Nearly half of the patients had come not for medical advice, but to congratulate me and wish me well. The medical consultations were mostly routine – winter coughs and colds – and regulars who came for monthly blood pressure or weight checks.

After surgery, I went for coffee with my partners. It was all back slapping, rude jokes about my engagement, and

7

advice from the three of them. They were delighted I was to be married, apart from the fact that, by and large, patients preferred married doctors.

Ron Towle was waiting to catch me when I came out from my coffee break. Ron was one of my poor disturbed patients, a loner who made his living with vague land and cattle deals. He took up more of my time than any other single patient.

Could he please see me just for a minute?

I mentally wrote off half an hour.

As soon as he came into my surgery he started to walk up and down, beating his chest. I had let him down. Where had I been? I was never there when he needed me.

Apparently, while I was away he had become more disturbed than usual. He had started to become abusive to his neighbours, and my partner, Jack Hart, had to have him forcibly admitted to Winchcombe Mental Hospital for three days to cool him off.

As usual with Ron's crises, this one was related to some business deal with which he was involved. He had bought some agricultural land that had a fair chance of being converted to building plots. Planning permission had been refused, and he now couldn't get the price he had paid for the land in the first place.

He was ruined. People took advantage. It was a plot. Those buggers on the Council had it in for him.

I let him go on for about ten minutes, then started to cool him down. It was another ten minutes before we achieved a normal rational conversation. I even managed to get him to laugh and, for a while, was able to persuade him that his business deal wasn't such a disaster after all.

I knew he would be back on the same tack the next day, or the day after, but I had learned to live with it.

'Now, Ron,' I said, 'I have some news for you. I have just got engaged.'

Ron was silent. He sat there, thoughtfully nodding his

head. Then he said 'You are a lucky, lucky man. It means you will get married and have children, and people will care about you.' He sat numb, more aware of his isolation than usual. 'You are a lucky, lucky man,' he repeated.

He got up slowly. His shabby old raincoat and frayed cuffs looked even shabbier than usual. He seemed small and crushed by all the indignities the world had heaped upon him. He turned when he reached the door. 'I hope you will be very happy, doctor,' he said, 'you deserve it.'

I sat thinking when Ron had left. Yes, I was very, very lucky. Did I deserve my good fortune? Perhaps not, and Ron certainly didn't deserve whatever mentality, chemistry, physiology, upbringing or environment which had created the situation he was trapped in.

The morning seemed to fly. I just had time for a quick sandwich before I started on the move again. There was a steady stream of visits all the afternoon, mostly to influenza victims.

Several patients were very ill. One man said his heart had been out of control in the morning. He was better now, he said, and all seemed well, with pulse normal and blood pressure normal – but on listening to his chest I couldn't hear his heart at all. It *did* seem that something could be wrong.

I discussed the case on the telephone with a very nice lady registrar at Winchcombe Hospital. I said I couldn't believe that my patient could have a pericardial effusion and seem so well. She said, 'Send him in and we will do a chest X-ray and electro-cardiogram and make sure.'

I was always pleased when it was a lady doctor 'on take' at the hospital. They are much easier to talk to. Or perhaps I just prefer talking to ladies anyway.

All turned out well in the end. I made a note to buy a new stethoscope.

My evening surgery started at five. A great number of children seem to come to evening surgery, it often being the only time one parent is able to bring them. There they were – with the usual infected ears, tonsils, colds and coughs.

Then all the myriad adult problems – indigestion, athlete's foot, shortness of breath. They wanted advice on family planning, on how to lose weight, how to put on weight. There were people who were worried about their children, and children who were worried about their parents; people who were worried about their jobs, and people who were worried that they hadn't got jobs; people who were just out of hospital and people who were just going into hospital; people who needed X-raying, and people who needed fairly complex investigation.

Surgery finished at 7.15 p.m. Home for a meal of bacon, eggs and beans again, and then, eight o'clock, my last Red Cross lecture of the series to the local detachment. It was finished. I went through a rough resumé of all we had covered during the course and to my surprise was given a box of cigars. A nice lot of people.

There were two night calls. 2.30 a.m. – a car crash. The driver had fallen asleep at the wheel – multiple bruises, no obvious fractures. Both occupants felt they were lucky to be alive – the car was a total write-off. Fortunately the only other casualty was a tree at the edge of the country road.

Four a.m. – the second call. Just when I was getting off to sleep. This time a twenty-five-year-old girl whose baby was delivered two-and-half months ago. She was now acutely depressed and had been weeping for twenty-four hours. There was no medical emergency here, but I read the anxiety of the family and had to swop my sleep for theirs.

The girl was sobbing, not talking, the house was alight and alive, and nobody was sleeping. Two boys were playing cards downstairs, baby was crying, sisters and brothers walking about. However many people lived here? I couldn't sort out all this girl's problems at that hour, but got her to swallow two sleeping tablets (I watched her to make sure she did), then sent everybody off to bed. I would see her tomorrow, when I knew she would have had at least a good night's sleep behind her. No, not tomorrow, it's already today. My main function had been to go along as an authoritative outsider and accept the responsibility for the situation. Now everybody could rest – someone else had taken over.

The weather had brightened the next day but after my nocturnal interruptions I came down rather bleary-eyed. There was more mail on my desk – investigation results, letters from specialists. All the partners saw all of the mail, thus keeping in touch with the developments of each other's patients. Gladys brought a cup of coffee, and slowly I felt like a human being again.

There were some surprises in the mail. One patient whom I thought was anaemic had such a high blood count that I suggested he became a blood donor. Another, who was just having some routine investigations, complaining of nothing really, turned out to be grossly anaemic and would have to be investigated further.

The surgery started at 9 a.m. The partners had an efficient appointments system and we avoided massive roomfuls of people waiting for hours. Not many appointments had been taken when I started, but by 11 a.m. I had seen twenty people: the usual coughs and colds and several being signed off to resume work.

Then came my biggest problems: depressed people and people under stress. This was – and is – the commonest single condition I had to deal with. It presented itself in many different ways. Sometimes a person was just feeling depressed, but more often feeling tired, run down and uninterested. It could take some time to ferret out that what was being presented as backache was really the cover for acute depression.

I once had a girl who attended surgery for weeks, complaining only of a painful thumb. Eventually I was able to find that her real reason for visiting was her fear of the physical side of her forthcoming marriage. She was to be wed in a few months' time, but was quite ignorant of what really happened – or was expected to happen – during the sex act.

I arranged for an interview with her and her fiancé together. We discussed the problem openly and, by facing it and exploring it, made it disappear. Her fiancé was a kind and considerate lad and the answer to their problem was for them both to be kind, considerate and patient with each other in the early days of their marriage.

The greatest problem in the treatment of depressive and anxiety states was my feeling of inadequacy. So often I could only treat the symptom. I couldn't change people's economic circumstances, couldn't find houses, new jobs or new marital partners. All I could do was support, listen, advise where it was appropriate, and sometimes prescribe anti-depressants or tranquillisers. These didn't help the fundamental problems but did lessen the anxiety, made it a little easier to cope and, by coping, to come to terms with, or solve, the problem. Sometimes the bereaved needed a tremendous amount of support and patience until they found their feet again. All I could offer was my compassion and a transfusion of my own energy. And this was not taught in medical schools. I wondered just how I would cope with the situations many of my patients had to contend with.

Other cases during the morning – a man of fifty-one complained of indigestion. As far as I could tell, on examination, his trouble was gastric, but there was a seed of doubt so I fixed up an appointment for him to have an electro-cardiogram. Mary, our dispenser, had been trained to use this machine and did her tracing by appointment in the surgery, or in the patients' homes if they weren't well enough to travel.

A few of the run-downs and feeling-tireds merited some investigation, and blood and urine samples were taken and put out to be sent to the Pathology Laboratory.

Then the usual light relief. Patients were always finding odd lumps they hadn't seen before when they were bathing or taking a shower. They were usually boils or simple cysts or fatty lumps, all innocuous. It meant, usually, sleepless nights thinking they had cancer, until they saw the doctor. They came in generally worried to death, and went out rejoicing. If I were asked what was the single most important thing a general practitioner did, I would have said it was to reassure, and he reassures with the weight of his knowledge of illness and its associations behind him.

I had got to know several people fairly well in my two years in Tadchester and knew, roughly, their behaviour patterns. It was helpful because I was able to notice if they started to behave differently. So, when Vera Vanston the Chairman of the Women's Institute, arrived in my morning surgery saying she felt like a gramophone that was running down, I thought there must be something wrong. Mrs Vanston rarely came to the surgery and was one of those seemingly inexhaustible women who had time for everything and everybody and, if she were not running every local organisation, would at least be a committee member.

She told me she was tired all the time, felt cold, was putting on weight, her hair and skin felt funny, and she just hadn't the energy or enthusiasm to tackle half the jobs that she normally got through without any trouble. She had tried slimming and all sorts of patent tonics, but was getting worse.

I had already made my diagnosis before she had finished giving me her history. When I examined her I found that she had put on weight since the last time I had seen her; her skin was coarse, the outer third of her eyebrows were missing, and her hair was thin and wiry.

'Well,' I said, 'your problem is a simple one. What is happening to you is that your thyroid gland is not as

13

active as it should be.'

The thyroid gland is very much like the air intake into a kitchen boiler. If it is left fully open it will roar away and burn up so much body fuel that you lose weight and become thin. This is what happens when the thyroid gland is over-active. When it is under-active (and this most commonly occurs in late middle age) it is similar to closing the air intake to the boiler, when the stove doesn't heat up enough and you don't burn up the body fuel, feel cold, and put on weight.

I sent a sample of Mrs Vanston's blood to the Pathology Laboratory, whose tests confirmed my suspicion that she had an under-active thyroid – myxcedema. Once having my diagnosis confirmed, I started her on thyroid tablets which she had to take every day to replace her deficiency. In three months Mrs Vanston was back to her old weight and figure, and leading all her organisations with the same zest as she had done before.

She called to see me at the surgery when she had been on the treatment for six months. I had never seen her looking better.

'Vera,' I said (we were old friends), 'you are looking marvellous, I only wish I were ten years younger.'

'Dr Bob,' she replied, 'you should try taking your own medicine – I *am* ten years younger.'

I had a second coffee at the end of what had been a very routine surgery, and was then off to do my visits.

Three calls for children with stomach pains. One for a sore throat. It *was* a sore throat, but closer examination showed it had been going on for some days. There was a mass of exudate on both tonsils and generalised glands all over. This was probably glandular fever, so I started the patient off on an antibiotic and took blood samples to clarify the diagnosis. It wouldn't make any difference to the condition; it would get better anyway. But I would then know whether there was glandular fever about in the district and on the patients' records they knew quite firmly that they did have glandular fever.

Of the three tummy pains, the two that might have been appendicitis turned out to be nothing, and the one who had diarrhoea (or who reported that he had diarrhoea) had had one small loose stool and presented as an acute appendicitis, so I had to send him off to hospital.

Two elderly patients. Both had a flare-up in their bronchitis and needed an antibiotic and some watching for a day or two. One of them was not too mobile and would need the district nurse to help her with her toilet and bathing.

Check calls on the two emergencies of the night before. The wife in the car crash had a badly bruised leg and a fracture had to be discounted, so I rang Winchcombe Hospital and fixed up an X-ray. Both husband and wife had found new bruises and were stiff and sore, but were thankful to have got off so lightly.

The sobbing young mother had slept well, but was still depressed and weeping. Her child was illegitimate and there was no supporting man in the background. A nice girl, and a lovely baby. She would get better and would survive, as people do get better and do survive. Nothing would improve at once, but the bad times would get less frequent. I could help her through the bad times with support and medication. I couldn't make them disappear, but I could blunt the sharp edges.

And so to lunch.

After lunch, just two ante-natals to be seen in the afternoon, then odds and ends – a medical representative, a cervical smear, and an examination for life insurance.

Ante-natal clinics are always pleasant things. Instead of people who are ill, there are healthy young mothers with something to look forward to. It is nice for a change to have medical conditions where there is a positive, happy end product.

Nurse Plank, the District Midwife, had both ante-natals all prepared for me; urine tested, blood pressures taken, and a reminder to me that another patient needed a further blood test.

Nurse Plank was one of the finest women I had known, a completely dedicated, caring midwife. She had never married, but nevertheless had thousands of babies she almost called her own. It was due to her skill alone that many of them were able to arrive in the world at all, and her caring did not just stop with the safe delivery of the baby; she was always scouting around for clothes, prams, etc. for the less well off. She gave advice and counsel to young mothers far beyond that required by her job. As I was beginning to find for myself, she had to give advice on house purchase, marriage, schools, and even such things as whether to buy a car. She never, to my knowledge, beat the request I had late one night when a mother rang to say her son had won a talent competition at Butlin's, did I think he should cut a record?

After seeing the ante-natals, a cervical smear. Again, everything was to hand. Nurse Plank had the forms filled in; instruments, slides and swabs were laid out for me, ready for use.

Next was my insurance examination. The patient grumbled at the fee of £4. I didn't really blame him for I knew just how he felt. We had just had a bill for £190 from our solicitors for drawing up a new partnership agreement.

I always felt rather sorry for medical travellers (pharmaceutical representatives). They used to have to sit about waiting for us to give them some of our time, then bring forth their latest wonder drug that was better than any other drug had ever been. I repeated my corny joke each time I had to interview a representative. I would examine his product, look intent, and then say, 'It must be good – the advertisements speak so well of it.' It never raised a flicker and I am sure none of them understood what I was getting at.

The medical representative would give us drug samples.

We would use them, then the patients who were given them would ask for more, so without meaning to, we had launched one more drug into circulation and the medical representative had achieved the object of his visit.

As I was about to leave the surgery a small boy was brought in. He had fallen off his pushcart and cut his head. With the help of Gladys, who stood by to pass instruments and cut stitches, I put three sutures in his head. He was terribly good, making no noise, and went on his way smiling after being rewarded with a sugar lump, very proudly wearing a bandage on his head.

Normally, on this day, I would have done a surgery at the boys' boarding school I looked after, but it was a half-term holiday and I had this extra spare time. I used that afternoon to catch up on some of my routine visiting of the elderly.

This was a most enjoyable area of medicine. Often the main treatment that you give elderly people, and the main medical treatment they require, is a visit. They just want to see a reassuring face come through the door, a reassuring face which has time to chat not only about medical conditions but about what is going on or, more often, about how things used to be. Most of the elderly people seem to miss the discipline of the old days. It is fine nowadays to do as you please, with no one looking over your shoulder, but in the old days there was always the Squire to go to if you had any major problems, and the Squire could, and did, give treats. Yes, they were better off than they used to be, but they did miss those treats when everything was arranged for them.

Young men and women in their early twenties, with spanking new sociology degrees, somehow were no substitute for the Squire, and I found it was primarily the doctor, the vicar, the health visitors and district nurses who had to bridge that gap.

Sometimes minor adjustments had to be made to patients' treatments, sometimes I would have to impose some new restriction.

It was very difficult to convince Mr Smith, aged ninety-three, that it was just not my lack of medical skill that was causing him more effort on his daily ten-mile walk. Bully for him! In all weathers I used to see him trailing round the country lanes with his stick.

There were some delightful old people of great age who had fought their lives' battles and, having survived that long, were gentle, philosophical people. I only wished I could spend more time over cups of tea, chatting over the cares and delights of the day.

The afternoon went all too quickly. A cup of tea, then back to the evening surgery, every appointment taken. There was never an easy surgery, and this one was delayed because, in the midst of it, a baby was brought in with a bad chest infection. I had to rush the child straight off to Winchcombe Hospital by ambulance from the surgery for immediate treatment. My surgery went on until eight o'clock, and I still had three calls to do.

Half past nine, home at last. I sat smack bang in front of my television set, my pipe firmly clenched between my teeth. Jack Hart was on for night duty, and unless someone came bleeding to the door I had an undisturbed night ahead of me. Woe betide anybody who should try and shift me from the box, regardless of whatever programmes might be showing.

My busy week had stopped me thinking too much about my impending visit to the de Wyrebocks' cocktail party. Sunday, the 12th, was in two days' time. They passed all too quickly. After a hearty breakfast I set off for the big house, prepared for the worst.

I rang the doorbell, and waited apprehensively. The door was opened by Commander de Wyrebock himself instead of the usual stone-faced butler.

'Come in, Dr Clifford,' he boomed, slapping me on the shoulder. 'I am damned glad to see you.'

The Commander was always pleasant, but this was a bit enthusiastic even for him, especially as on my last visit he had all but thrown me out. I was sure Mrs de Wyrebock wouldn't greet me with the same warmth.

I was led into a room where there were about a dozen of the County Set, all elegantly dressed and just as elegantly sipping sherry. I knew only a few of them by sight; the rest looked like relatives.

Mrs de Wyrebock detached herself from the group she was talking to, and came towards me. 'Now for it,' I thought.

She walked straight up to me, smiling, and kissed me on the cheek. 'Delighted to see you, doctor,' she said, 'though I hope we may call you Bob from now on – or do you prefer Robert? I thought we would just keep it family this morning. Don't you agree?'

A sudden terrible unease began to creep over me. What in God's name was happening?

The various males in the party one by one detached themselves from their various partners and came over and growled 'Congratulations' or 'Every happiness', always in rich, fruity, blue-blooded voices.

I was no longer uneasy about what was going to happen next – I was scared to death.

'Bob dear,' said Mrs de Wyrebock, 'Marjorie won't keep you a minute. She does feel she wants to look her best, and she is so excited.'

This couldn't really be happening. I was in the middle of a nightmare. Why wouldn't the alarm clock go off?

Marjorie didn't keep us waiting long. She came bursting in, and I had to admit she didn't look too bad. The Tadchester beauty salons must have been better than I thought. Her hair was done nicely, she was skilfully and tastefully made up so that the outline of those teeth was a little less horse-of-the-year than usual.

To my horror, Marjorie walked straight over to me, as her mother had done, and kissed me on the cheek.

'Isn't this all absolutely spiffing?' she said. She gripped my hand then, turning to the assembled company, said in the loud voice that she used to rally the Pony Club at gymkhanas, 'Ladies and gentlemen, I have an announcement to make. Dr Bob, this dark horse here, and I have become engaged.'

I felt the world beginning to collapse around me.

CHAPTER 2

I couldn't remember proposing to Marjorie even in my
most drunken moments. And anyway, I hadn't seen her
for weeks. Feebly, I began to protest. She cut me short
and went on, 'Dr Bob is an old and dear friend, and we
all depend on him. I hope you will all treat him as one of
the family. The great coincidence is that he became
engaged on New Year's Eve, the same night that Paul and
I became engaged. It was such a coincidence that I
wanted to share my engagement announcement with him.
Now I would like you all to meet my fiancé, Paul
Charteris.'

Through the door stepped a huge ape of a man of about forty-five, smartly dressed, obviously County and belonging, and with one particular physical characteristic – he had teeth that were even bigger than Marjorie's!

I nearly fainted. I knew then how relieved they felt at Ladysmith.

The rest of the party passed in a haze of champagne and the whinny of horsy voices. Eventually I got away and drove home, completely exhausted. I felt as if my whole life had just flashed before me. The sooner Pam and I were married, the better. I couldn't stand too many shocks like this.

My shirt was soaked through with perspiration. I was having lunch with some farmer friends – Janice and Kevin Bird – and had to go home and change before I went on to them. I arrived late and exhausted. They collapsed with laughter when I told them my story.

'Come on, Bluebeard,' said Kevin, 'get stuck into some prime rib of beef. It will settle your nerves.'

After lunch we drove to Sanford-on-Sea, and walked along the beach. It had been raining in the morning, but a watery sun broke through in the afternoon, and the walk along the beach, well wrapped up against the cold, blew the fears and the remnants of the morning champagne away.

Kevin and Janice were great friends of mine and had put Pam up on her two brief visits to Tadchester. Eric, my other close friend and companion on most bachelor expeditions, was keenly courting a girl called Zara. The bachelor days for both of us were numbered.

Zara was a tall, artistic-looking blonde who drove round in a Morris Estate car with a pet owl on the top of the back seat. I would defy anyone to guess her occupation. She dressed beautifully and at parties looked as if she had stepped straight out of the pages of *Vogue*.

Zara was employed by the county council – as a rat-catcher. She must have been the most beautiful and exotic local Pest Control Officer any council had the good fortune to employ. Jeremy, her owl, was never short of a supply of fresh meat.

I bumped into her once when we were both visiting the same farm.

'Look at my haul for the day,' said Zara. In the back of her estate car she showed me a sack containing some one hundred and fifty dead rats.

'None of these for Jeremy, poor old thing. I've poisoned this lot.'

Zara once disgraced herself at a farm when she was attacked by a prize rooster. To fend it off, she took a swipe at it with her heavy metal poison spoon, and neatly decapitated it.

There was litigation between the farmer and the county council for weeks, and we teased poor old Zara unmercifully.

'Look out, Eric,' I would say, 'she might easily decapitate *your* cock.'

Every week I would make some time to have a cup of tea with my old friend Bob Barker at the second-hand bookshop at Sanford-on-Sea, near the slipway. He was one of the nicest, wisest old men I have ever met and always kept a box of small cigars in his desk drawer so that he was able to offer me one on my visits.

I could sit and listen to him talk for hours about old local families and the landed gentry; how there was always one of each generation of these families who carried the inherited spark of success. They would become prosperous businessmen, politicians, or military men. However unlikely a particular litter looked, there was always one who carried the vital gene that kept him in the uppermost group of men of distinction and property.

He would point out other successful men as being the bastards of various members of the aristocracy where perhaps some parlour or dairy maid had spirited the winning line away from a family.

He was delighted to hear of my engagement.

'Women, Bob,' he said, 'I have never understood. I have had what is called as successful a marriage as anyone has had. We have brought up a happy, healthy family, and have grandchildren and great-grandchildren. Then, one day,' he said, with a chuckle, 'a few weeks after our golden wedding three years ago, I was watching my wife bustling round the house. She has been a marvellous wife, mother and grandmother. The house is meticulously clean, she never forgets a birthday, and she's a wonderful cook. As I watched her, I realised that I had never known her. She was a stranger I had lived happily with for fifty years. I never ever knew what real thoughts went through her head.

'I realised, looking back (and it was only when looking back that I saw it), how badly and inconsiderately I must have treated her at times. I was so concerned with myself and my music, my books, my importance, my relationships with other people, I just don't know whether she ever noticed or minded.

'I often think about it. Once or twice I have tried really to get to know her, to know how she ticks, but I have never got anywhere near. After fifty years, she still surprises me sometimes.

'That could be the secret of a successful relationship – marry someone who never ceases to surprise you . . .'

He took out another cigar and pushed the box across the desk towards me.

'I think,' he said, 'that there is a group of people who would make a successful marriage with whomever they happened to settle with, and another group of people who could only make a marriage with one specific person, a twin soul.

'I have never known which group I belong to, but whichever it is, I have been lucky. As well as that,' he said, 'I have enjoyed and loved my music.' (Bob had been

24

the organist at Tadchester Parish Church for forty years.)

'I have learnt some things, but somehow, the older I grow, the less I seem to know. One of the things I have learnt, and knowing your agnostic views you must excuse me for using the Church as an analogy, but,' he said, with a twinkle in his eye, 'the successful church is the one whose organ fund has never closed.'

I would have to work that one out.

'That's enough of an old man pontificating. Today is a special occasion; whether you are on duty later on or not, you are going to have a glass of Madeira wine with your cigar.'

Old Bob was a gem. I wish I could have recorded all his anecdotes and our conversations. I was always encouraging him to write his memoirs but he said he was not a writer, although his whole life had been spent among writers.

Before moving with his wife and daughter to the semi-retirement of his second-hand bookshop at Sanford-on-Sea, he had for many years had a flourishing bookshop in Tadchester itself. It had been a focal point for Somerset and West Country writers. He had had a small dining-room at the rear of the shop where he held literary luncheons and introduced writers to publishers. Many a struggling author had been advised and encouraged by Old Bob if, indeed, not supported by him.

He talked without bitterness of a most successful author, now a household name, who for years came to him for free meals, loans of manuscript paper, money, advice and support. 'I even once,' Old Bob said, 'gave him three of my shirts.' As soon as this author had become successful, he left Old Bob's little circle, never bothered to keep in touch, and did not even pop in and see him when he was visiting Tadchester.

Duty called, and reluctantly I tore myself away: I could have stayed all day with Old Bob and his twinkling advice.

'The successful church is the one whose organ fund has never closed.'

I just couldn't get it.

There were many things I couldn't get. I could never get over the fact that I was not always my patients' first choice as their doctor. I would work extremely hard over a patient to get him through some particular illness only to find that, as soon as he was better, he would attend one of my partners. It was no consolation to me that he had been attending this particular partner for years before I had treated him. I couldn't understand why anyone who had been cured by me should ever have another doctor. I must have been one of the most supreme egotists in my early days.

Miss Harmer and Miss Chesterman helped to cut me down to size. They lived a few houses down the road from Miss Gill and Miss Booth at Sanford-on-Sea. Miss Gill and Miss Booth were great friends of mine and were remarkable for the fact that although Miss Gill had been bedridden for nearly fifty years, looked after by Miss Booth, she had led one of the most full and successful lives that I have ever known. They were inundated with visitors and Miss Gill said 'The thing is, doctor, people come to see me because I have time to listen.' We were good friends and I knew that they prayed for me, which always gave me a twinge of conscience.

I never reached quite the same closeness with Miss Harmer and Miss Chesterman, although they were sweet old ladies and never had a bad word for anyone. The set-up was both similar and different. Miss Chesterman was obviously a lady of means and Miss Harmer was a paid companion/help, though at the time of their life that I met them it was impossible to tell who helped whom.

Some time before I came to the practice in Tadchester, Miss Chesterman had been very ill. She had been looked after by my predecessor, Dr Cookes, who had resigned from the practice before my arrival because he could not keep up with his self-inflicted pace of work.

There was no doubt that Dr Cookes was a fine doctor. His patients adored him. He was selfless in his time and devotion to them and he was a good clinician, but he was probably the first man to admit, in truth, that he couldn't see the wood for the trees.

Miss Chesterman and Miss Harmer could do nothing but sing his praises.

'Do you know, doctor,' they would say, 'sometimes on his Sunday off, Dr Cookes would spend more than two hours here and we used to say to him, "Shouldn't you be back at home with your wife?"'

Nobody could live up to this sort of devotion, including Dr Cookes, who just couldn't meet the demands on his loving care that he himself had created and encouraged. He retired and went off to Canada where, I expect, being the man he was, he would re-create the situation he had just left.

If he had been able to make a proper charge for his services, then his time ratio per patient would not have mattered quite so much. But from what I heard of him he would find it very difficult to ever present anyone with a bill. A lovely man and, as is the nature of lovely men, in hard, crude, commercial terms his own worst enemy.

I looked after Miss Chesterman and Miss Harmer for many years. They both had rather poorly hearts. Miss Chesterman had repeated chest infections and I was a constant visitor, but never on my Sundays off. And never did I – could I – spend two hours with them, even when they were ill. Eventually one of Miss Chesterman's chest attacks was too much for her and she died, cared for to the last by her devoted companion.

After a few months I managed to get Minnie Harmer into an Old People's Home where she soon settled down and was loved as the gracious, selfless person she was. Some years later, when I was married with a family and

Minnie was well into her nineties, she came to spend Christmas Day with us. She was marvellous, telling us all her life history. The gold locket hanging round her neck was given to her by her previous master and mistress for devoted service, which only ill health had caused her to give up. She worked for them for twenty-five years and she had retired in 1911.

It was 1961 when she came to have Christmas lunch with us. She loved the Christmas tree, my mother, Pam my wife, and the children. She was gracious and amusing. I drove her back to the Old People's Home at Sanford-on-Sea. She had had a lovely day and sought to pay me the greatest compliment that she could. 'Well, doctor,' she said as she got out of the car and I helped her into the Old People's Home, 'Miss Chesterman and I were right about our first impression of you. We both said that you would be the nearest we would ever get to Dr Cookes.'

I smiled to myself. This was accolade.

Fifty years ago Tadchester was one of the most important fishing ports on the Somerset coast. A feature of the town was the fishing boats unloading on the quay, with the locals queueing up to buy fresh fish straight from the boats. As in many other coastal areas, the fishing industry had dwindled and Tadchester was left with one fishing trawler going out regularly, one fishing trawler going out intermittently, and the salmon fishermen, who fished for salmon in the estuary with their nets.

There were two fresh-fish shops in Tadchester. One was owned and supplied by the Hadcock Brothers, who owned the only full-time fishing trawler. Les, the eldest brother, ran the shop, and Jack and Charlie did the fishing. The other fish shop received its supplies from Billingsgate, one hundred and fifty miles away in London.

The Hadcocks were all patients of mine; fine men, whose family had fished the waters of the Somerset coast for many years. They were steady men, devout Methodists, but not without a sense of humour. Jack, the middle brother, was the cleverest of this generation of Hadcocks. I liked them all, the two fishermen especially.

'When are you coming out on the boat with us, Doc?' said Jack. The thought of twelve hours out at sea, trawling, appealed to me.

Eventually we fixed a day which suited both my medical timetable and their fishing programme, and I set off with Jack and Charlie in their trawler, the *Lady Alice*. We chugged down the Tad to cross the bar three miles out of Tadchester, by Sanford-on-Sea, then into the open sea.

I felt very manly and nautical standing by Jack in the wheelhouse, but didn't like too much the smell of diesel oil drifting up from the engine-room.

I had not taken anything against sea sickness; although I am not very good about moving over the water I felt confident travelling in local waters. Going down the Tad, where there was not a ripple, confirmed that this was the right decision.

Once over the sand bar that protects the mouth of the estuary from the ravages of the sea, the boat started to pitch slowly up and down in the swell, but still this didn't appear to bother me.

'Well, you have got a good day for it, Doc,' said Jack. 'We won't get a much calmer day than this.'

I began to feel a little bit queasy when we had been out in the open sea for about an hour. The boat began to roll more as Jack and Charlie commenced to pay out their net. Half an hour later, with a further slight increase in swell, I was definitely much more than queasy – I was green.

'You had better lie down in the cabin for a bit, Doc,' said Jack.

The two brothers were fully engaged with their fishing. I went and lay down in the small stuffy cabin. It smelt of fish and diesel oil and I felt awful. I stuck it for quarter of an hour, then came back on deck. I had just reached the side when I started to be as sick as I had ever been in my life.

In between the bouts of sickness, I lay down by the side of the boat wishing I could die. Jack and Charlie were far too busy with the winches, running the boat and getting their net out, to be bothered about me.

'You will be all right, Doc,' they said. 'Sorry we can't help you.'

I looked at my watch. I realised with dismay that, with the tides as they were, there would be another eight hours before we could turn round and head for home.

The day seemed endless. Jack and Charlie did three long trawls and seemed to collect mountains of fish. While they were trawling, they got to work on gutting and cleaning the fish of the previous haul. This didn't help me one bit and their offers of soup and coffee only encouraged me to make more visits to the side. I could quite happily have jumped into the sea and finished it all, even with the knowledge that I had only a few more hours to stick it out. Thank God there were no press gangs any more. It would have meant an early and untimely end for me.

I tried to sleep in the shelter between the boatside and the cabin, and did eventually doze off. When I woke up, I felt somewhat better and the boat had lost its undulating movement. I raised my head above the side, to see that we had crossed the sand bar and were chugging up the Tad. Half an hour and we would be home.

Strange: I felt better as suddenly as I had felt ill earlier.

Both Jack and Charlie were concerned about the bad day I had had, but coming up the river I even felt well enough to tackle my sandwiches and Thermos of soup before we finally docked.

'Thank you for the day out,' I said to Charlie and Jack. 'It has helped me to lose a few pounds if nothing else.'

'Oh, don't let this beat you, Doc,' said Jack, 'you must try it again.'

The defeat and shame of my day with Jack and Charlie hung over me. I felt people were smiling at me behind my back, as even strangers began to come up to me and ask how I had enjoyed my day's fishing.

I resolved to go again, but this time I kept clear of diesel fumes, filled myself with anti-sickness pills, and had a most glorious day out, with the sun shining and hardly a ripple on the water. I helped with the net, even gutted some of the fish between hauls, was ravenous for my Thermos and sandwiches halfway through the day, and was allowed, with Jack's guidance, to steer the boat home over the bar and set it chugging up the river.

They grinned good-naturedly as I got off this time, with a bag of fish to split between my partners.

'I knew we would make a fisherman of you,' said Jack, 'we might even sign you on as a regular hand.'

I thought that, having regained my ground, I would probably leave it at that, particularly as the next day there was a Force 8 gale and the weather was so bad that Jack and Charlie had to ditch one of their nets and head for home.

With our Seine net fishing on the beaches, I did at least always have one foot almost on the ground.

The River Tad was well known for its salmon, and the Tad salmon industry was a very profitable one. However, through over-fishing, particularly by the estuary nets, the number of salmon caught gradually diminished. The salmon rods, which were extremely expensive further up the non-tidal part of the Tad, were not only costly but unrewarding. But the idea of a spell of salmon fishing was so attractive to the people in the bigger towns that they would spend a lot of money on a fruitless fortnight talking about the ones that got away. It did give them the kudos of being able to talk about the salmon stretch they had hired that spring.

One could while away a very pleasant hour in the afternoon standing on Tadchester Bridge; watching the commercial salmon fishermen shooting their nets in the bridge pool at low tide was fascinating. With one end of the net on the shore, the rest piled up in the stern of the boat, the boat would be rowed out in a huge circle, the piled net being paid out as they rowed. When the boat touched shore again, a circle of floats a quarter of a mile in circumference marked where the net lay. Then, with two men on either end of the net, one on the top rope and one on the leaded bottom rope, the net would be slowly and systematically drawn in. Watching from the bridge, one peered down into the dark water, trying to see if there was anything in this haul (*draught* was the proper word).

As the last corks reached the side of the river, activity could be seen in the bunt (end of the net) and the last portion of the net was quickly and carefully hauled up the bank. Long silver shapes could be seen thrashing about, entrapped in the bunt. The netsmen clambered over them, hitting the heads of the fish with short lead pipes, killing them instantly.

There was usually something in each haul. I have seen as many as twenty salmon brought out; beautiful fish, weighing between five and fifteen pounds, lying on the bank. The catch usually included a few sea trout, some small flat fish, and the occasional mullet.

Net fishing in the estuary had a long tradition. Someone was making a lot of money out of it. The general public saw only what was taken out during the day; just as many fish were obviously taken out at night. Occasionally I would be left one of these great-beauties in the surgery by a grateful patient or by a patient who hoped to get a sick note that he was not fit enough for work – which meant he had a licence to go net fishing.

One more aspect of the fishing scene was unfolded to me when Gladys popped in at the end of one spring evening surgery and said 'Sorry, Doctor Bob, there is an extra patient who insists on being seen. I have tried to get him to go up to the hospital but he won't go, and his language is appalling.'

Gladys blushed and for Gladys to blush the language must be really rough. The Thudrock colliers never drew a line between what they called 'pit talk' and how they asked for prescriptions and appointments in the surgery. Gladys coped with them all right, so I waited for my 'extra' patient with some interest and a little trepidation . . .

CHAPTER 3

There was a knock at the surgery door. Before I'd time
to say 'Come in', in walked a big man, wearing a tweed
hat, anorak, and tweed trousers tucked into a pair of
wellington boots. He walked stiffly, with his right hand
clutched to the corresponding buttock.

'I'll have to shake hands with me left, doctor,' he said as
I greeted him.

'Fine by me,' I said. 'Won't you sit down?'

'If it's all the same to you,' he said, wincing slightly, 'I'd
rather stand.'

It was John Denton, River Authority head bailiff on the
Tadchester end of the River Tad. Born and raised in the
industrial North, his love of fishing and the outdoors

had taken him away from the smoke, out into the country, and eventually to what he termed, 'T'last bloody 'ole God ever made' – Tadchester.

Though he had been away from the North for nearly twenty years, he had not lost his accent; in fact the longer he had been away, the thicker it had become. His favourite words were *bloody*, *bugger*, followed closely by *sod*. These words, in richest Mancunian, could be heard nightly in the Tadchester Arms and contrasted strongly with the fruity accents and public school vocabulary of the pukka salmon and trout fishermen, and with the West Country burr of his local cronies.

John, in other words, was a character. Big, bluff, boozy, but a dedicated bailiff and angler; as ready to take a youngster patiently through his first attempts with a rod as to put the toe of his large right wellie into the pants of a poacher.

And now he had a problem.

'I've had 'em in some bloody funny places before now, doctor,' he said. 'But this bugger beats all.'

He turned around and lifted his anorak. There, dangling from the seat of his pants, was a large piece of pink metal. 'It's a Devon minnow,' said John – a salmon lure. It was dangling from a vicious triangular hook which had obviously gone in much further than the tweed.

'Eh, don't *you* soddin' laff,' he said. 'I've had enough o' that from them daft buggers down at the river. Especially the one who put it in me with his cack-handed castin'. He soon stopped laffin' when I threatened to put a gaff up his jacksi . . .'

I gathered from this information that the lure was being used by an inexpert angler whose skills John had been attempting to improve, and whose first cast had been made before the coaching had taken effect. I was relieved that John had not put a gaff up his jacksi, or I really would have had a busy morning. (A gaff is a butcher's-

35

sized hook on a handle, used for lifting out beaten salmon, and jacksi is a non-medical term for that part of the human anatomy which is roughly bull's eye when viewed from a posterial elevation in a subject who is touching his toes.)

'All right, John,' I said. 'I promise not to laugh. Now take your anorak off, and bend over with your hands on the seat of that chair.'

John did so, and I felt gingerly around the point at which the hook had penetrated. His thick trousers and some thicker undergarment defied accurate diagnosis.

'I'm afraid I'm going to have to spoil your trousers, John,' I said.

'Feel free, Doc. Supposed to be thornproof tweed, these bloody things. Pity the buggers weren't hookproof as well.'

With a small pair of scissors I cut a circle of cloth from the trousers, and a corresponding one from the thermal long johns I discovered underneath. I then shredded both circles to clear the hook – or rather, hooks.

A treble hook is just that: three hooks mounted back to back at angles of a hundred and twenty degrees to each other. Two of the hooks had penetrated John's buttock beyond the barbs. Once a hook has penetrated beyond the barb, it can't come out the way it went in. The only thing for it is to cut off the end of the shank, and then push the hook through the flesh, point first. John manoeuvred his trousers and long johns down over his gigantic rump so that I could operate unhindered.

'Want an injection, John?'

'Nay, lad. Yer'll no doubt be givin' me some anti-tetanus or anti-fowlpest or some such when yer've done. Just dab a bit of freezer on it an' I'll grit me teeth.'

John gritted his teeth, and apart from a smothered 'Jee-sus Christ!' as the second hook came out, he uttered not a word.

It was quite a neat job, though I do say it myself. Just

two pinholes where the hooks went in, and two more where they came out. I cleaned and dressed the spot, gave John his anticipated anti-tetanus jab, and stuck a large plaster over the inside of the hole in his trousers so that he could face the world without embarrassment.

'Thanks, doctor,' he said. 'I'll get back to t'river now and see who else that daft bugger has maimed. If he's crippled any of his mates, I'll send 'em on to you. Tek 'em on as private patients – and charge 'em plenty . . .'

. . . At evening surgery, John was back again.

'Trouble?' I asked, trying desperately to think of any complications which might have set in. Surely lightning could not have struck twice in the same place.

'No, Doc,' he said. 'I just brought you summat, that's all. Didn't want to leave it outside for everybody to see.'

From under his anorak he pulled out a long, newspaper-wrapped parcel and plonked it on my desk.

'Good 'un, that,' he said. 'Fifteen pounds, fresh-run. Until this afternoon she were still in th'watter.'

It was a salmon: a beautiful, silver, spring salmon. On its flanks were half a dozen sea lice, the hallmark of a fish fresh-run from the sea.

'John,' I said, 'I'm overwhelmed. I really don't deserve this just for treating a . . . a – '

'Pain in the arse?' said John. 'Nay, lad. Get it down yer. It'll do yer good!'

I bumped into John quite often after that. Sometimes, after evening surgery or a round of calls, I would call in at the Tadchester Arms for a quick pint before going back to the flat, only to have a large scotch plonked in front of me by the barman.

'That's on Big John,' he'd say. And there would be John, either further down the saloon bar giving the benefit of his wisdom to some tweed-clad game fishermen, or winking through the hatchway from the public bar, where he would be engaged in more earthly conversation with the Tadchester locals – some of whom I recognised as acknowledged poachers.

John was very friendly with Jack Dawson, the timekeeper at Thudrock Colliery. One day, in a moment of weakness, Jack confessed to me that his secondary job as a part-time hangman gave him back trouble and I had had to issue a sick note to the Home Office stating that I felt his hanging duties were bad for his back.

These two huge men were a formidable combination and most people went out of their way to keep on the right side of them. Jack had been a professional boxer. It was only strangers to Thudrock who ever risked getting into a punch-up with these mighty two, and they always found that they had chosen the wrong side.

'Get it down yer, Doc,' he'd say. 'It'll do yer good . . .'

I didn't have the heart until much later to tell John that I didn't really *like* whisky. I always seem to have been blessed, or cursed, with a whisky drinker's face – whatever that is – and John was only one of many patients who assumed that the Doc liked nothing more than a hefty scotch.

The bailiff-poacher relationship puzzled me until I realised that such a situation was often the case with men operating on opposite sides in the same field of activity. Certainly it was so with the local police and the local villains, and with the local ex-soldiers and their opposite numbers. One summer the Tadchester British Legion played host to a party of German ex-servicemen: ex-Desert Rats and ex-Afrika Korps men toasting each other and swapping stories in boozy evenings at the Legion Hall, and everybody having a whale of a time.

'It's like this, yer see,' said John, one evening when I'd asked about the company he kept. 'The local lads know me and I know them. If I catch them on my beat, they know they're in for a belting. But they're only doing what I would be doing in their place. And they give me the nod if we get any outsiders coming down after the fish –

sometimes they'll see 'em off for me, and that saves a lot of trouble.'

Organised gangs of poachers from outside Tadchester were one of John's big problems. They would come down from as far away as London or Birmingham in Land-Rovers with nets, poisons, gaffs, snares, snatching tackle and wicked three-pronged fish spears. Working at night they would operate by flashlight, or even small search-lights. Working quickly and moving from pool to pool they could strip almost every resting salmon from quite a long stretch of river.

John had had several brushes with them and had twice been badly beaten up – he now rarely went out at night without Jack in tow.

'There's not a lot you can do when you're on your own against half a dozen hard cases. Nowt except mebbee make a lot of noise and hope you've frightened them off. I've given up wading straight in and trying to nab 'em. My name's Cupid, not Stupid.'

Warned by local poachers of an impending raid by a gang from outside, however, John had been able to move in once or twice with a scratch posse of these same locals and a couple of constables, and bring a gang to court. John never knew, nor did the police, how word of a gang's impending arrival worked its way into the Tad-chester local villains' grapevine, but he knew when not to ask questions.

Another of John's pet hates was the system of licensed netting at the mouth of the Tad. Local fishermen were permitted to operate with nets during the salmon runs and to take a specified and limited number of fish.

'Limited be buggered,' said John. 'One feller there entered twenty-one salmon on his catch record, and I was there when he brought his boat in. There were a hundred and fifty fish if there was one. That part of the river was outside my beat, so there was nothing I could do except bring in the police – and if you've tried waking the buggers up in Tadchester after midnight, you'd know what a fat lot of good that would be. The bloke would have been off and gone with his fish before the local Flying Squad had got on his bike. Apart from which, the netsmen don't take kindly to interference, and I've grown quite fond of me front teeth.'

There was quite a bit of the poacher in John, as there is in most gamekeepers. One morning in March, I was taking the air by the banks of a brook which ran into the River Tad, before facing morning surgery. Walking the other way, a haversack slung over his shoulder, was John.

'Mornin', Doc,' he said. 'What are you after – a couple of trout fer yer dinner?'

'No, John, just taking a breather. Shouldn't think there'd be any trout in this brook anyway – it doesn't look wide enough for sticklebacks.'

'Don't you kid yerself, lad. Here, hold me bag.'

From the haversack John took a short-handled landing net, and cut a stick from a hedge nearby. He waded into the stream – never went anywhere without his wellies, didn't our John – and pushed the net into the water under the overhang of the far bank. With the stick in his other hand, he thrashed the water about four feet upstream of the net.

When he pulled out the net, it held two thrashing brown trout. After a quick smack on the head each with his priest – a small weighted club – he laid them on the bank and tried again further upstream. Just one trout this time. A little further up – another one.

'There y'are, Doc lad – two fer thee and two fer me. Nowt like a fresh trout unless it's two of 'em.'

'Thank you very much, John,' I stammered, amazed at the speed of the operation and even more amazed that there were any trout in the brook at all. 'But isn't this – er – sort of against the rules?'

'Aye . . . yer could say that,' said John, slipping his

brace of trout into his haversack and slinging it over his shoulder. 'But just you wait until you taste the buggers . . .'

Now and again I would be called in to do a post mortem on a case of drowning. There were always several in the holiday season and most of them were straightforward, but one puzzled me. The body was found in fresh water, beyond the tidal reach of the Tad, yet the water in the lungs was salt. No foul play was suspected – the person concerned was last seen alone walking the rocks on the beach just before an incoming tide – and it was put down to a freak of the currents: the drowning was in the sea, and yet somehow the body had found itself well upriver.

It puzzled me for months, and one day I mentioned it to John.

'Oh, aye,' said John. 'And was it found by a boatman?'

'Yes,' I said, and mentioned the name of a local fisherman.

'He were daft to use a sea drownin',' said John. 'But you'll get a few which finish up a long way from where they went in. It were an offcomer, that one.'

He explained that for bodies found in the water within the local authority area, a reward of £3 was paid to the finder. For bodies found on the beach, or for those up-river under county jurisdiction, nothing was paid – so enterprising boatmen who found a body would tow it to the stretch of the river where some cash was to be had. 'Offcomers' as such bodies were called by the locals, had contributed to the beer money of Tadchester boatmen ever since the statute granting the reward was enacted in 1887.

John was a great raconteur. One of his favourite stories was about The Brother Who Got Religion.

Two Scottish brothers came to fish the Tad for a week, both expert salmon fishermen. One of them had recently contracted a bad attack of religious mania. He wore rough

41

wool next to his skin, ate only the plainest food, drank only water, ignored the comfortable hotel bed and slept on the floor, and prayed every three hours on the dot through the day and night.

John had pointed out a decent salmon lie to the brothers and left them to it.

After a while, Jamie – the 'normal' brother – hooked a huge salmon, thirty pounds if it were an ounce. He played it for half an hour and eventually got it near enough to the bank to gaff it.*

'Angus!' he shouted. 'The gaff! Quick, man!'

There was no reply. The salmon bucked and streaked off back into midstream. Jamie used all his skill to play the fish back to the bank.

'Angus!' he screamed. 'The gaff! For God's sake, man!'

Again there was no reply.

Jamie turned his head to see Angus at the top of the bank, kneeling with eyes tightly closed and hands clasped upon his breast. It was the three-hourly prayer time. And, salmon or no salmon, Angus was praying.

The salmon bucked again on the tight line and leapt clear of the water. This time Jamie was not quick enough to release enough line to absorb its lunge. The line snapped like cotton – and the salmon was away.

'The last I saw of those two lads,' said John, 'was Jamie streaking across the field waving the gaff and screaming Scottish war cries – and Angus breaking the four-forty-yard record for holy men . . .'

The poacher in John certainly helped him to recognise the poacher in others, even the most unlikely looking.

One of the regular salmon fishermen on John's beat was a highly respected member of the Tadchester community:

---

* The gaff is now banned on many waters, especially early in the season. Many anglers today, anyway, prefer to use the tailer – a wire noose on a handle – to bring in the fish, by looping it round the 'wrist' of the tail. But in those days the gaff was generally used.

prosperous fishing-tackle dealer, Rotarian, JP, and author of countless articles in the angling press in which he extolled the virtues of the salmon and the vices of those who took them by unfair means. His name was Smeaton; he carried himself with a military bearing, spoke in the clipped tones of one born to command, and insisted on being addressed as *Major* Smeaton.

Sitting as a magistrate, he was given to lecturing offenders on decency, discipline and the British way of life. He obviously modelled his delivery on Field Marshal Montgomery and talked a lot about 'straight bats' and 'hitting you people for six' ('you people' being whichever miscreant happened to be before him).

He was especially hard on anybody accused of poaching or breaking the fishing bye-laws on the Tad. Too hard, in John's opinion, and for a while John took only the most serious cases to court.

John did not trust the Major. There was something shifty underneath that brisk manner, and something strange about the Major's bags of salmon. He could catch fish when nobody else on the river could – including John – and would wring the last ounce of publicity from his feats. After a particularly bad fortnight on the river, during which the Major had bagged half a dozen salmon and nobody else had had so much as a bite, John was pondering his success in the Tadchester Arms.

'Only one thing would make them buggers bite this week,' he said, 'and that's putty. I'd swear he was using . . . eh, by God, that's it – the bugger's using putty!'

The use of 'putty' – salmon roe – as bait was highly illegal, but difficult to prove. The putty was soft enough to come off the hook in the water as soon as the angler jerked the rod, so a putty user would strike – pretending he had a bite – as soon as he saw the bailiff . . . and all that would be left would be the lure around which the putty had been squeezed.

One afternoon in January – with still a week to go before

43

the salmon season began – John noticed the Major's car leaving the river bank and heading for the road. John was near enough to head it off while it was still on River Authority land.

('Might have been dodgy if he'd got on to t'road, lad,' said John later. 'I wouldn't have been within me rights then.')

'Mornin', Major,' said John.

'Ah, morning, Denton. Nice day, what?'

(The 'Denton' bit offended John's North-country sensibilities. He had a handle to his name.)

'Beautiful day, Major. And the river's running well. Plenty of fish moving already, I gather. Been spyin' out the land fer next week, have yer?'

'What? Er, yes, Denton. Spying out the land. Exactly. Looking out some promising lies. Nothing like a spot of reconnaissance, as we used to say. Patrolling in depth, what?'

This didn't impress John, who knew that the Major's finest hours during the war had been spent with the Pay Corps in darkest Manchester.

'You won't mind if I look in your boot, will you Major? Purely routine. Got to get into practice, like.'

'I certainly would mind!' snapped the Major. 'Now be a good fellow and get out of my way. I've an urgent Watch Committee meeting to attend!'

'Won't take a second, sir. And you can tell t'Watch Committee you've been setting a good example.'

'Now look here, my good man! . . .'

That did it. Big John was nobody's good man. His tone became quiet, which was always a bad sign.

'I've got the right ter force this boot, Major. And I'd rather not mek a mess of a gradely car like this. If yer wouldn't mind, I'll 'ave them keys . . .'

The Major handed over the keys, his mouth set in a tight line under his clipped moustache. Inside the boot was just a waterproof fishing cape.

44

('When I saw that,' said John, 'I thought I was for it. Mood 'e was in, me feet wouldn't have touched.')

John lifted the cape. Underneath were six salmon. All fresh run, none under twelve pounds and the biggest a handsome twenty-pounder. And the season was still a week away.

'Now look here, my man,' thundered the Major, exploding into one last bluster, 'you'll be in very serious trouble for this! There's a perfectly logical explanation!'

'I know,' said John. 'I know. You left the boot open, turned yer back for a second and the buggers jumped in and closed the boot after them . . .'

In spite of his contacts in the town and on the Bench, the Major was heavily fined and banned from the water for a season. Before the season was out, he had sold his tackle business and moved to Scotland to open another one.

'Think yerself lucky,' said John, as the Major raved at him outside the courtroom after the case. 'If I'd have had owt to do wi' it, yer'd have been banned for life – *and* got six months like any other poor bugger.'

When the Major finally left town, John was troubled by remorse. Under his bluff, tough exterior, he was really soft-hearted and didn't like doing anybody down – even though the Major had got far less than he deserved.

'Yer see, Bob lad,' John said over a pint in the Tadchester Arms, 'it wasn't so much that he was using putty – thought we couldn't touch him for that. It was that for years he'd been such a bloody hypocrite.'

I knew what he meant. John himself was no angel – but at least he had never pretended to be . . .

To some forms of poaching, John turned a blind eye. Another respected pillar of the Tadchester community, well into his fifties, had fished the river since he was a boy with only moderate success. He lived in the shadow of his long-dead father, whose skill with a rod was legendary and whose obsession with salmon was total. The son had inherited the obsession, but not the skill.

He used to tell a story of how, as a boy, he had seen his father play a salmon into shallow water over a gravel bank. The salmon had leapt from the bank about ten feet into a nettlebed higher up. His father had dropped his rod and dived into the nettlebed after the fish – but the salmon had leapt again, snapped the line and somersaulted back to the river and freedom.

I heard the sequel to this story, not from John – who never breathed a word of it – but from the Tadchester businessman himself, who came into the surgery with a streaming cold about a week after the incident.

He was walking along the bank one day, towards the spot where his father had had his famous encounter. Suddenly, right in front of him, a salmon leapt clear across from some way out and landed in the shallows over the gravel bank. Something snapped in the businessman's brain.

'It was like Moby Dick,' he said. 'I was convinced it was the same salmon – after forty-odd years, the *same fish* – and I owed it to my father's memory not to let it escape this time.'

Immediately he dived into the shallow water – clad in bowler, pin-stripe suit and clerical-grey raincoat – and grabbed the salmon. It flipped from his hands back into the water and then, with a mighty flick of its tail against the gravel bottom, shot straight up the bank into the same nettlebed.

The soaking-wet businessman followed, screaming, 'You got away from my father, you swine – but I'm damned if you'll get away from me!'

There was a titanic struggle among the nettles, the thump of a rock on bone, and eventually the businessman emerged, soaking wet, covered in mud and incipient nettle rash, and with a three-foot-long bulge under his raincoat.

John greeted him as he reached the road.

46

'Bit dampish today,' said John.

'Er . . . yes, John,' said the businessman. 'Silly me. I slipped and fell in.'

'Anything' movin' in the river?' asked John, as if the sight of a dripping and muddled pillar of society were the most normal thing in the world.

'Not a lot, no. In fact . . . er . . . not a thing as far as I could see.'

'Well you get yourself home,' said John. 'Before you catch your death.'

Next day, the businessman bumped into John again.

'Nice fish you had yesterday,' said John.

'What?' said the businessman. 'How did you – er – that is . . . blast it, why didn't you book me?'

'Any man who would go to that much trouble for a fish deserves all the salmon he can get,' said John. 'And besides – who'd have believed a bloody silly story like that . . .'

CHAPTER 4

Ante-natal clinics are happy, healthy places. Obstetrics is the one branch of medicine where there are truly happy endings, a positive end product rather than just a restoration of the status quo.

It is only very occasionally today that childbirth is marred by the death or disease of either mother or baby. It happens so rarely in fact that one tends to disregard it as a possible factor in a birth.

I made a mistake in one case, to some extent a justifiable one – and one which did not involve any real tragedy – but still a mistake.

Gertie Shaw was a big, fat, pleasant woman. She had a ten-year-old son and longed to have a second child. She was huge. Her starting weight was something in the area of twenty-five stone, and when she appeared at my ante-natal clinic she had already increased this by another fourteen pounds.

Pregnancy tests of patients' urine in those days were unreliable and expensive and not undertaken very often, and apart from early diagnosis there did not seem much reason to do so: Nature, in time, always demonstrated quite clearly whether a woman was pregnant or not.

Gertie Shaw came in, beaming, saying she was four months pregnant. She certainly looked pregnant: on the other hand, I could never remember a time when she didn't. Her pregnancy was confirmed by the fact that she had ripe breasts, prominent veins round the nipples and was already beginning to secrete some milk. She had a huge abdomen that externally was just a huge abdomen; I was unable to palpate anything through the thick layers of fat. Attempting to perform a vaginal examination was impossible: her thighs met somewhere just above her knees and I had no idea what was really going on inside. I wondered how she had managed to even conceive at all.

Pregnant she was without doubt. She claimed she was four months gone, calculated from the time her periods stopped.

Gertie put on weight exactly as she should have done, even a bit more. Each month she showed an increase of six or seven pounds, her breasts increasingly produced milk (which is the case with some expectant mothers at an early stage). She had no sign of a period and although I could not – as I would normally do – hear the foetal heart through the thickly padded walls of her abdomen, she assured me that the baby kept her awake with its kicking and this was a real lively little one.

She continued to progress well until about four weeks before she was due to be confined. I had booked her into St Mary's Hospital as her home facilities were poor. Not having any idea of the size and shape of the baby nor, in particular, which direction it was pointing, I sent her for an X-ray.

She came gleefully to the next ante-natal clinic, asking 'Is it twins, doctor?' I had been teasing her for a long time, saying that it must be at least triplets, she was so huge. But I had some awful news for her: the X-ray was completely blank.

Gertie had what is called a phantom pregnancy. (She had some famous predecessors, including Mary Tudor and Marie Antoinette.) Her wish to become pregnant again had made her body follow the signs and symptoms of pregnancy. If she had been ten stone lighter, I could easily have excluded a real pregnancy, but her sheer weight and bulk prevented me from making any proper assessment. With the wonderful intruments that we have nowadays, such as ultra sound, it would have been no problem, but these were not available then.

There had been no doubt in either of our minds that she was soon going to have her second desired offspring. She had cashed her maternity grant; she had bought a pram. Everybody knew she was expecting. She had become one of the close family of mothers, the exclusive club that forms amongst pregnant women. It is a close and warm circle.

I had to explain the situation to her as gently as possible. Not only could she not believe it, but she was left with the problem of what to do. She was now nearly twenty-eight stone, with a giant belly and huge, sagging breasts. The whole family, the whole street – in fact almost the whole town – was looking forward to her delivery. She was beside herself with frustration, disappointment and wondering how she would be able to face the outside world. She swore me to secrecy and we formed a plan that she would go home to bed and stay there.

Gertie kept her maternity grant. It was rumoured (and the rumour was never denied) that she had lost the baby.

Somehow, behind her closed doors (she would not let even me in for the first weeks), she sat down and starved herself. In four weeks she had lost five stone, and everybody accepted that she had been through the tragedy of losing a baby.

She was able to sell her pram with some dignity, and we kept her secret: in fact she rather enjoyed the fuss and sympathy she of course deserved. Sympathy she got – she had lost a child, a much loved and cherished one too. It was such a pity, it *would* have been much loved and cherished.

Ante-natal clinics had other surprises to offer, mainly related to the appalling, and sometimes frightening, lack of knowledge that mothers-to-be had about reproduction and childbirth.

There was one patient who had put a piece of Elastoplast over her navel, convinced that she was suffocating the baby. Another was sure she was pregnant for the first time but would not allow me to examine her because she was in the middle of a period.

Mrs Yvonne Petranger was a tall, slim, smartly dressed woman who lived in a modern split-level house overlooking the estuary and was a member of Tadchester's small, hard-drinking, sophisticated set. Her husband was a car salesman or, rather, a garage owner, and had garages both at Winchcombe and Tadchester.

If I were awarding a prize for lack of maternal knowledge, there is little doubt but that Mrs Petranger would be a strong candidate for first prize. She had spent the first five months of her pregnancy in Winchcombe and had now come to Tadchester, where she wished to be confined. I did not know what the medical standards of her general practitioner in Winchcombe were, but there were no records of blood being taken for blood grouping and anaemia tests, or of the other usual routine investigations that one does in the early part of pregnancy. All that had been recorded were a few blood pressure levels and a pregnancy test on Mrs Petranger's urine, showing that she was actually pregnant.

I was obviously going to have to start at the beginning.

Nurse Plank, the midwife, snorted with disgust when she saw the notes of the Winchcombe doctor. She was meticulous about her midwifery; she lived for it, and was loved by what must have been thousands of mothers whom she had seen through childbirth. I knew that if I dared put a foot wrong she would be on me like a ton of bricks.

We had some difficulty getting blood samples from Mrs Petranger. 'Is it really necessary, doctor?' she asked. It took some fairly sophisticated chit-chat before we managed to persuade her that it *was* essential. The actual sticking of a needle into her arm and extracting the blood turned out to be a major operation.

'Now, let's have a look at you,' I said.

She went behind the screen and got undressed and lay on the couch. I came round to examine her.

'Doctor,' said Mrs Petranger, 'I wonder if you would mind checking. My mother is a bit small in her outlet and had some difficulty in being delivered. She thinks I might be the same. I would be very pleased if you could check that for me today. My husband would really like me to go to a private clinic in Winchcombe but I asked if I could see you first – they say you are so good with mothers and babies.'

'Certainly,' I said. I was going to do so anyway, it being part of my general examination.

She smiled. She had obviously chosen her doctor well.

I put on a rubber glove to do an internal examination, and lifted the sheet off her stomach. She was still wearing a pair of small black briefs. I said 'You will have to take those off, Mrs Petranger.'

She looked puzzled and, slowly and reluctantly, took

them off. She lay back, looking mistrustful, and watching me cautiously.

I put some antiseptic jelly on my gloves, then reached for the lower part of her abdomen in an attempt to do an internal examination to assess the size of her pelvis and whether she was likely to have any difficulty with the delivery of her baby. As my hand began to make contact with this rather vital area, Mrs Petranger shot up, screaming, pushing my hand away as if I were indecently assaulting her (which I expect I was in a way), shouted '*Not there, doctor!*', and collapsed in tears.

The hardbitten, sophisticated, well-dressed Mrs Petranger knew very little about the facts of life. She must have had what was almost an immaculate conception as her virginity had not been completely destroyed, and Mr Petranger must have completed his fertilisation at a fairly long range.

Somehow she had arrived at the age of twenty-eight thinking that when babies were born they were delivered through the umbilicus. It took an hour of patient explaining, tears, and a cup of tea, to tell her what the whole thing was about.

'You won't tell anybody, doctor, will you?' she said.

I had come across Mrs Petranger's situation before, as a medical student when we had a gynaecologist's daughter who had the same way of thinking.

In cases of infertility, where couples had been trying unsuccessfully to have a child, I learnt in time before I did any investigations to check exactly where, and how, they were trying to conceive. Somehow the navel, to a small minority of people, has a magic of its own, and I knew of at least three couples who had fruitlessly tried to pursue this as the route of conception.

Mrs Petranger gave up all thought of the Winchcombe private clinic after our first frank discussion on the route by which babies entered the world.

She had a normal pregnancy, but a fairly rough delivery; she could not co-ordinate her pushing very well and eventually I had to do a forceps delivery in St Mary's Maternity Home, with Jack Hart dropping chloroform and ether on the other end.

Before I put on the forceps I had to complete the small operation required to eliminate the remnants of her virginity.

I had a word with her husband after delivery about their marital life.

'I can never get near her, doctor,' he said. 'She is always running away from me. She doesn't like sex – she is frightened of it – and I understand that her mother was the same. Will it be all right now she has had a baby?'

'Yes,' I said, confidently, knowing full well that there was no longer any barrier to prevent her husband making headway.

I discussed Mrs Petranger's case with Steve, my senior partner. He told me that, in his experience, alas, this situation was not uncommon, but the birth of a baby too often may not be the end of a couple's physical difficulties. Somewhere along the line there may be some inbuilt psychiatric damage. To resolve it would require a lot of patient psychiatry which, frequently, the patients decline to have.

'But for some,' he said, 'the birth of a child resolves all their physical problems, and they go happily on from there. I hope that the Petrangers fall into this group.'

Pam and I fixed 9th September as the day we would get married. The wedding would be held in Leatherhead, and we had seven months to fix all arrangements and for me to find some accommodation for us. The flat above the surgery was far too small for two and we could not afford to buy a house, so I set about finding somewhere to rent.

Eventually I found a first-floor flat in a three-storey house Up-the-Hill. It stood on its own in about a quarter of an acre of garden; the large ground-floor flat was occupied by some Americans who were tenants of the owner of the house and we were to be sub-tenants of Herbert Barlow who rented the top two floors and lived alone in a room on the uppermost floor.

Herbert Barlow, as I came to know him over the years, was one of the most remarkable and memorable men I have ever met. He claimed to be a gentleman, a writer and a man of the theatre, and he was without doubt the most available man I have ever known.

He looked like a writer, sounded like an actor: a stern dignified face, carefully groomed silver hair, and a deep resonant voice that trotted out theatrical platitudes, punctuated with growling 'my dears'. He had a perfect set of teeth.

He looked, and was, a man acting a part. Through all the time I knew him I fluctuated from thinking that he was a complete sham to joining in with him and saying the right words and lines. He lived frugally, explaining that when his last marriage broke up he decided to dispense with possessions, leaving himself free to dash off to the south of France, New York or Italy if anybody required him.

He said, 'I don't have any dependants now and I don't intend to be dependent on anybody else.'

There was no doubt that he did write, for in his little room there were five fully prepared manuscripts of plays on his desk.

'Once I get a couple of these on in the West End I shall be made. Look at dear old Maugham [Herbert considered Maugham was an intimate and an equal], he had exactly the same trouble, and finally had five plays on at the same time.'

These plays were always *nearly* being produced. Herbert would say 'Dear old A is interested,' dropping some theatrical household name, and I would pretend to believe him. One day when I was with him in his room, the phone rang, and there *was* old A asking for Herbert and obviously knowing him, but somehow his plays still never got produced.

In all, I knew Herbert over ten years, during which time he wrote twelve plays. His manuscripts, beautifully prepared, could not be bettered; they included intricate stage directions, and for some of them he built elaborate model stage sets.

I read them all. For the very professional way they had been prepared they should have been produced. On picking up the manuscripts and folders one knew immediately, as when one first met Herbert, that these were professional plays, written by a professional and a man of the theatre. But on reading them they seemed to be all dialogue and manuscript, stage directions, lights, props; there was no story, no characters emerging, and I could never understand what he had been trying to say until he explained them himself.

Herbert used to talk of his days before the war, in the south of France. 'My natural home, old boy.' He was then a film script writer and living on half the income he was receiving. 'Went there to die, old boy. My dear friend Dr X, who is now a medical superintendent at The Great Y Hospital, said I had consumption, coughing up blood, thought I had only six months to live.'

This was the kind of hackneyed, classical melodrama around which all the episodes of Herbert's life seemed to revolve. 'One of the biggest disappointments of my life at that time,' he said, 'was Daisy, half of a famous dancing sisters act. We had been living together for eight years. As soon as she knew I was ill, she left me. Eventually she married Lord Z.' Anyone connected with Herbert couldn't possibly have married into anything less than the peerage.

'Do you see your friend the doctor at all now?' I asked.

'No, old boy, haven't seen him for years. He married again and I just couldn't get on with his wife. If I was ever

56

ill though I would, of course, go straight to him.'

Any of the important people Herbert knew were at all times just out of reach. They were, without exception, intimates, but there was always some reason why they would never be in touch with him; either they brought back old memories, or there was some area of friction such as a new life, or he didn't want to get in touch with them until he was once more re-established in the theatre.

'Of course,' he said, 'the war finished my stay in the south of France. Had to come back to England.'

It would have been typical of Herbert to say that the Government had sent a battleship to rescue him in the teeth of enemy fire, or that he had at least swum from Dunkirk, but he never gave an account of the circumstances of his return.

What was certain was that, at the beginning of the war, he was the manager of a large London theatre. He talked about the royalty he had entertained there, about the private film shows for the prime minister, how he was on intimate terms with them all. Coupled with these stories of his association with such people, his theatre, and his writing achievements, were his stories of daily triumphs in the local market where he had got a penny off coffee, twopence off cheese, or found a remnant of material from which he could make a shirt.

He had bought an old sewing machine for £2, and could make any type of wearing apparel – he made a shirt for me, and an evening dress for Pam.

I am sure that sometimes he went hungry. He had no visible means of support, other than some occasional play 'doctoring' for ambiguous theatre companies. 'Plenty of money backing this, old boy,' he would say. 'They have asked me to make something of it.' I saw two of these plays.

Having his manuscripts typed cost money. Posting them cost money. He used to say, 'I have a couple of hundred pounds capital, old boy, but don't like to touch it.' I was never able to bring myself to believe this.

He claimed to have stage managed sometime or other every London theatre, starting after the first world war at the old Alhambra Theatre with 'Bing Boys on Broadway' and the Diaghilev Ballet.

Herbert tucked himself away in his top-floor room with his memories, his manuscripts and his great associations. Life was as simple as possible – in his room he had only a bed, a desk, two armchairs and a double gas ring. He used to come down to our flat for his weekly bath. A devoted daily called Elsie came and 'did' for him and took no payment for her services; she adored him and always thought of him as a great man.

He had so arranged the domestic pattern of his life that he was ready at a moment's notice if he should be required by a theatre or film company. 'I could pack and be off for six months tomorrow if they needed me, old boy,' he would say. He even didn't like being out of the district in case he missed a call that he knew one day would come – the call that would lead to the success which so far had eluded him.

Of the ten years I knew him, the last two he spent fighting a terminal illness that would have finished most people in six months. During those two years he wrote a spiritual play which was to be the climax of his life and work. He finished his play and sent it round, but it had the usual rejection slips. Nobody was interested. Obviously, although he had been a very good stage manager and could improve other people's manuscripts, he just couldn't write plays himself.

He was getting much weaker now, so I took it upon myself to get in touch with his great friend Dr X, super-intendent of The Great Y Hospital in London, and to my surprise Dr X was a great friend and offered to take him straight into his own hospital and give him full VIP treatment.

Herbert's health was failing so rapidly that I knew he

would never attend another first night. Unbeknown to him I contacted some of the great men of the theatre he had mentioned, explaining the position and the importance to Herbert of his last play. Again to my surprise, they knew him and all had a great affection for him. He had been a successful film script writer and a well-known stage manager.

The friends and I got together, and one of the more influential of them wrote to Herbert saying how much he liked this last play and that he hoped to produce it at some date in the future – a date, we all knew, when Herbert would no longer be there to help with the stage directions.

Herbert accepted this letter calmly. 'I knew, old boy,' he said, 'that there was a purpose in my struggling on these last two years. I know this play has a message,' and his eyes shone with triumph from his now gaunt face.

Herbert died with dignity as I knew he would. I contacted those relatives I could find and, having perhaps been closer to him than anyone else, offered to help pay the funeral expenses. But Herbert had left £200 in the bank – enough for all the expenses, and some left over for Elsie who had worked for him for nothing for so many years.

On the desk in my study I keep a pile of beautifully prepared play manuscripts in a cardboard folder, tied round with a piece of brown ribbon. Nobody will ever produce them, but they are my memorial to my great friend, Herbert Barlow, Gentleman, Writer and Man of the Theatre. A man who always kept himself available, never realising that he had spent so much of his life pretending to be the sort of person he actually was.

CHAPTER 5

Tadchester continued to surprise me with the unusual characters that kept bobbing up.

One morning, returning from a 6 a.m. call I came across Ivy Henshaw struggling across Tadchester Bridge with two large suitcases, off to catch the early morning bus from the terminus. I drew up and offered her a lift, which she gratefully accepted.

'I think I would have missed the bus without you, doctor,' she said.

Ivy had been the usherette at the Tadchester Picture Palace for as long as anyone could remember. She was the Queen of the Upper Circle and Balcony, and ruled her little empire with good nature and a loud West Country laugh. She was a big girl, with poor eyesight, but in the gloom of the cinema she could recognise and name nearly all her patrons.

Outside the cinema she led a very quiet life, living in a small house in Quay Street, a tiny street off Bridge Street in the centre of Tadchester. What she lacked in intelligence and education, she made up with good humour. She lived quite alone, but kept an eye on and did the shopping for the young crippled man who lived next door to her. Sometimes, on a Sunday, I would see her having her weekly treat – lunch in the quayside snack bar.

'Now, where are you off to, Ivy?' I asked.

'Poland, doctor,' she replied.

I thought she was joking. I would have put Ivy's maximum range as a package coach trip to Plymouth or Torquay or, at the most, a couple of nights in London.

'Are you really going to Poland, Ivy?' I asked.

'Oh, yes, doctor.'

'Is it a package holiday?'

'No.'

'Do you know anybody in Poland?'

'No.'

'Well, why are you going?'

'Oh doctor,' she said, 'I go somewhere different every year,' and she told me her story.

Ivy's local accent was so broad that it was very doubtful if anyone who lived more than ten miles away from Tadchester could understand what she was saying, but for two or three weeks every year she would go off to a new country and somehow find her way around it. She told me that she had gone to Russia the previous year, Spain the year before, and was going to Poland this year. She hoped, perhaps, that Bulgaria might have something different next year. 'I didn't like those Spanish trains,' she said.

As we drove to the bus station, I discovered that Ivy's method was just to book her flight or train to whatever

61

country she had an inclination to go to. Then, on a very limited budget, without any knowledge of any foreign language, and with her almost unintelligible English, she would manage to travel round and find accommodation in this new country.

She didn't seem at all concerned about this trip to Poland. I tried to imagine her talking to booking clerks in Spain, Russia, and Poland; at reception desks in foreign hotels and boarding-houses. I couldn't imagine how she did it – but I could have hugged her . . .

Two weeks after dropping her at the bus station, I received a card. It was a picture of some Polish square, with a cobbled road and tramlines running through it. It read:

Dear Doctor,
At the moment I have seen Wrzesnia, Konin, Lowicz and Poznan. Just left Zola, Zowa, Wola, birthplace of Frederick Chopin. The 18th-century country house stands in a beautiful park and is now a museum. Thanks for the lift to the bus depot. Ivy.

For the first time I thought about how people from this small crowded island that I lived on, at one time colonised and administered about half the world. It was people like Ivy going forth, oblivious to difficulties – language, financial or otherwise – who had founded that vast empire. A few Tadchesterians would have maintained it quite happily and would have thought nothing of it.

A month later Ivy came to my surgery, full of beans, sporting an engagement ring on her finger.

'Did you have a good holiday?' I asked.

'Marvellous,' she said, 'and look, doctor, I am engaged. It is a Polish count.' (I felt certain Ivy would settle for nothing less.) 'He was the porter at the hotel I stayed in in Warsaw. Do you think you could give me some tablets to lose weight? We hope to get married in six months' time, and I want to lose a stone or two before then.'

I talked to Ivy about her diet, and gave her some amphetamine tablets, which would not only restrict her appetite but would give her a bit of 'get-up-and-go' which would help in getting rid of some of her excess weight. Somehow I had an awful feeling at the back of my mind that the marriage would not come off. I don't know why: Ivy seemed so happy.

A month later Ivy returned. She had lost nearly a stone in weight but no longer wore her engagement ring.

'What has happened to the count?' I asked.

'Oh,' said Ivy, cheerfully, 'when I wrote to him it was his wife who replied. He was married all the time, and she said his ring was worthless. I think he must have got it from one of those little crane machines.'

She seemed quite unmoved by her emotional disaster.

'I would like some more of those tablets if I could, doctor. I've been roaring all over the place since I started them.'

I gave Ivy another month's supply and cautioned her not to exceed the prescribed dose.

When I first went to Tadchester, 'soft' drugs were unknown, anyway by name. We knew of – or at least had heard of – heroin and cocaine addicts in the big cities and were beginning to suspect that pethidine, which was pretty freely available, should not be prescribed too often.

Barbiturate sleeping tablets, and the stimulant amphetamines, were in everyday use. It was common practice to take an amphetamine stimulant if you had a night drive or you needed to keep awake for some specific purpose.

I was then Medical Officer to the Tadchester Forward Medical Aid Unit. This unit, which consisted of a doctor, a trained nurse and eight members of St John's or the Red Cross, composed a team which travelled round the country successfully competing against teams from the larger towns.

To both settle my team and give them a bit of 'gee-up' before entering competition arenas (we usually had forty or fifty made-up casualties to treat in the middle of a large hall) I would often give them a Drinamyl tablet. No one suffered any obvious ill effect, and we usually won.

Nowadays, such has been the abuse and misuse of drugs like the barbiturates and amphetamines, you would be breaking the law, and could actually be prosecuted, for just having some in your possession. In the good old, bad old, days of my early years in practice, barbiturate sleeping tablets and amphetamines were widely and usefully used. If you were overweight, you were given a long-acting amphetamine tablet to reduce your appetite. (I shudder when I think of how such treatment would be viewed now.) Sometimes, in addition to the appetite-depressing amphetamines, we prescribed thyroid tablets to help burn off surplus fat.

Widow Cox was one of my constantly overweight patients. She regularly came for amphetamine tablets to suppress her appetite, but each month (Gladys used to weigh her on each visit) she hardly ever varied. She might be a pound up one month, or a pound down the next, but she made no impression on her basic fourteen and a half stone.

I had almost given up the battle. She swore she didn't eat large meals, but on two occasions at least, I had seen chocolate wrappers sticking out of her handbag.

One Thursday she came to my surgery for her routine monthly check a completely changed woman; a change, unhappily, for the worse. She had obviously lost weight but, in doing so, looked ten years older. On checking the weight slip, I found that Widow Cox, whose weight had been stationary for at least ten months, had dropped by twenty-two pounds in just four weeks.

'Well done, Mrs Cox,' I said. 'This is marvellous. How did you manage to do it?'

'Oh, doctor,' she replied, 'whatever have you done to

me? Why did you make me take the tablets at night instead of in the morning? I haven't slept for a whole month. I feel a complete wreck.'

I knew perfectly well I had never prescribed slimming tablets to be taken at night, but Mrs Cox had been taking them just before she went to bed. On enquiry, the reason wasn't hard to find.

When I was writing prescriptions, if I wished a tablet to be taken in the morning I wrote 'OM' beside the number of tablets I was prescribing; if I wished tablets to be taken at night, I wrote 'ON'. In the turmoil of a busy day, my N's and M's were not always too distinguishable.

Mrs Cox had had her prescription made up at Neville's, the chemist's shop in the town; somehow it must have escaped his proper scrutiny. I had to explain to her how the mistake had been made and make sure her next prescription was clearly marked 'OM'.

The next month Mrs Cox reported back, bright and breezy, her old self again; in fact, exactly her old self again! She had put back the twenty-two pounds she had lost the previous month. As soon as she had stopped taking the Dexadrine tablets each night, she slept for three days and nights, then got up and bustled around.

We went through her diet together. No, she hardly ate a thing. No breakfast, hardly any lunch, and just a bit of supper. 'In fact,' she said, 'if I didn't take a couple of bars of chocolate each day for energy, I wouldn't be able to keep going. I think my glands must be wrong, that is what is making me overweight.'

I stopped Mrs Cox's tablets. We were obviously not making any headway, but I continued to keep an eye on her weight. To my surprise, the next time she came to the surgery, four weeks later, she had lost seven pounds. This weight loss continued each month without any help from me until she was down to a trim figure, with no weight problems at all. I wondered how she had done it.

The answer came to me one Sunday afternoon on Tadchester quay. There was Widow Cox walking along the quay, dressed in her Sunday best, on the arm of a tall, thin, angular man. Widow Cox was courting. It was obviously a much better cure than any of my tablets.

Poor, sweet Miss Jessie Braithwaite was the opposite to Mrs Cox. She had never had a weight problem but one afternoon when I was visiting her sister, whom she looked after, she did confess to me how badly she had been sleeping recently. (Her sister Ethel had a bad heart that we were able to keep under control providing she did not overdo things, but an attack of bronchitis had overstrained her heart and I had had to insist that she have a spell of bed rest.)

Jessie's problem had started at the beginning of Ethel's illness. She had been up for two or three nights, had her sleep pattern disturbed, and not been able to drop back into a regular sleeping habit since.

I explained to her that the commonest cause of insomnia was having formed a habit of staying awake. If she took a course of some sleeping tablets for a few nights, she would form a regular habit of sleeping again and all would be well.

I gave her half-a-dozen pills from my bag, assured her of a good night's sleep, and told her I would come and see her sister the next day.

The next day I found both sisters in bed. Miss Jessie, who was rarely ill, was completely incapacitated with a bad back.

'Now, Miss Jessie,' I said, 'have you been trying to lift your sister?'

'No, doctor,' said Jessie. 'My bad back is through your tablets.'

Apparently poor Miss Jessie had taken my advice and taken one of my sleeping capsules, a barbiturate, about an hour before she was due to go to bed. She slept soundly, and woke to find herself fully dressed, lying halfway up the stairs. The action of the tablet had been far too swift for her – and her backache was caused from the hard edges of the stairs sticking into her back through the night!

Troubles arose with both amphetamines and barbiturates when patients started to mix them with alcohol. Alcohol made both more potent. Not only did it add to the effect of the barbiturate sleeping tablet; it resulted in its being absorbed much more quickly. A moderate dose of barbiturate plus a moderate tot of alcohol could combine together to form a lethal mixture, and a number of untimely deaths were recorded throughout the country where people had taken sleeping tablets after having had a few drinks.

Similarly, alcohol and amphetamines gave all sorts of bizarre results. People behaved strangely and out of character – there were accounts of people walking out of windows at parties, being aggressive and acting in all sorts of strange ways. With both barbiturates and amphetamines, users could reach a stage where they could not do without them and would beg, rob, or even kill, for their drugs. The dangers were recognised and thus, over a period of years, two valuable medical drugs were gradually withdrawn from use by the general public.

Pam and I had fixed our wedding day for 9th September at St Mary's Church, Leatherhead. There seemed to be a tremendous amount to do and Pam came to Tadchester as often as she could. I had arranged to take over the flat from Herbert Barlow in April; from then on Pam came down every other weekend and managed to spend a whole week in Tadchester at the beginning of June.

The Harts were always very kind and provided her with accommodation. We were closely chaperoned and although we tentatively suggested that I could sleep on the settee in my flatlet, or we could put up a camp bed in Herbert Barlow's flat, it was gently pointed out to me that this sort of thing was not approved of in Tadchester.

Tadchester was largely Methodist. There were in fact two Methodist churches, one in the High Street and one in Mill Street. This did not mean that the other churches did not have their adherents. There was one Congregational church, one Baptist, and about six others of various shapes and sizes, like the Unitarian, Christian Scientist, Free Gospel and Tabernacle, apart from a staunch Roman Catholic element and, last but not least – in fact, the biggest of them all – the Anglican church which was big enough to merit having a prebendary rather than a vicar as its minister.

I looked after at least a dozen ministers of religion of different sorts. The Church had a great influence on the community; it was said in Tadchester there was only one certain way of getting on the Council, and that was by being a Methodist.

Pam was awe-stricken at her first meeting with Herbert Barlow. His voice dropped a few octaves when he spoke to her, rumbling away in his most austere tones. Did she know the de Quinceys in Leatherhead? One of the richest families in England. Great friends of his. She must send them his regards when she got back.

As I started paying rent for the flat from April, Pam was free to come and measure for curtains and carpets; she had me putting up shelves, painting and wallpapering. It was a large first-floor flat – two huge reception rooms with Claygate fireplaces, a small guest bedroom, a large double room for ourselves, and a large kitchen/breakfast room. The bathroom was communal in the fact that we had to provide a bath once a week for Herbert and Miss Gulliver – not together: Miss Gulliver had the three rooms on the top floor not occupied by Herbert.

In addition to paying the rent, we had to buy some furniture which had been left there. At one time Herbert had lived in the whole flat with one of his wives (presum-

68

ably his last). In the bedroom was a huge, ornate double bed with a padded headboard and attached wing cupboards. The bedroom suite had come from a film set, and Herbert told us that Marlene Dietrich had lain on the bed during some film whose title he could not remember. I could hardly wait to get to bed! There was a wing-back armchair in the lounge that Herbert had made himself, and in the dining-room a dining suite which matched well enough and, in fact, was very good furniture. There were Regency chairs, a sideboard that looked as if it were Sheraton but was in fact a very good one from Maples' store, and a polished dining table, all hallmarks of the dignity of Herbert's past.

Much of each weekend was taken up in introducing Pam to local people. She loved Bob Barker at the bookshop, and thoroughly enjoyed her formal tea with the de Wyrebocks. If I had been asked to name two ladies who had nothing in common, I would have said Pam and Marjorie, but in fact they got on extremely well. They both had their forthcoming marriages in common. Marjorie was getting married a week before us and Eric and Zara, who had become engaged, were getting married a month after. Pam and Zara became the best of friends and arranged a couple of shopping trips in London on weekends that Pam did not come to Tadchester.

Frank and Primrose Squires took us Seine net fishing, with Joe and Lee Church making up the party. It was to be Pam's initiation into the art. Frank had his own net with which we trawled the beach at Sanford-on-Sea at night, hoping to catch sea trout and various flat fish and bass. Frank was the land surveyor for the county council – a real outdoor man – always shooting, fishing or sailing; a born leader, with an infectious humour. Joe Church was the games master at the local grammar school.

Usually five or six of us took the net out. It was about sixty yards long, had a pole at either end, with traces like those on a dog sled leading off from each pole. With one man on a pole at either end of the net, holding it upright, and as many volunteers as possible pulling on the traces from the pole we would trawl parallel to the beach in as deep water as possible with the outer pole (outer staff) ahead of the inner pole so the net trawled parallel to the beach like a letter 'J', the idea being that the men on the outer staff would drive the fish into the bulging bottom of the 'J'.

On Pam's first night just the three of us took it out, Frank and I on the outer staff, with Joe on the inner. It was really hard work. We could only slowly move the net along through the water, and the girls had to help us pull it up the beach once we got clear of the sea. We had one of our best catches ever, several sea trout, which were stuffed in jumpers and pockets in case the Water Bailiff saw us, four large bass, some mullet, about a dozen skate and various flat fish.

Every couple of hundred yards we would pull up the beach – these were called draughts – and any fish in the net were mercifully killed by a bang on the head with a piece of lead piping, then thrown into a little box on runners which it was the girls' job to tug along the beach.

The box filled rapidly and the girls complained how difficult it was to pull, offering to swop places with us in the water while we pulled the catch.

We decided to trudge back with the catch whilst the girls went for a midnight swim. They had no costumes with them and as we got some distance away, we could hear their giggles through the darkness. They were obviously going to swim in the suits that Mother Nature had provided.

The box was heavy and we were a good three quarters of an hour trudging back to the cars. We dried ourselves, changed, and sat waiting for the girls, periodically flashing our torches to show where we were. About a quarter of an hour later they came running up to us. We sat round, drinking coffee, eating sandwiches and talking.

Pam went to the car to fetch a rug and came back in tears.

'Oh, Bob darling,' she cried, 'I seem to have lost my engagement ring.'

This was awful. We had covered miles of beach so the chances of us finding the ring were very small. We set off back across the sand, following our footprints and sled marks, towards the sea's edge.

After walking for ages the marks in the sand suddenly took a right-angled turn, the point where we had left the girls. To our absolute delight, there, winking up from the sand in the torch beam, was the diamond in Pam's ring. Our chances of finding it like this must have been thousands to one.

Pam clung to me with relief.

'You've got a right one there,' said Frank. 'When she decides to bathe in the altogether, it is really in the altogether, she doesn't even wear a ring.'

Wearily, but happily, we turned round and trudged back to the cars.

CHAPTER 6

In winter, Tadchester was a rugby town. The local rugby
club turned out five sides each Saturday and the main
winter social events were associated with the splendid
clubhouse and bar that the club had built for themselves.

To produce seventy-five young men each Saturday the
club had to have a pool of one hundred and fifty players.
Many of them worked on farms or had other occupations
that meant they were not available every weekend.
Added to that were the inevitable injuries, weddings,
funerals and christenings that all took their toll.

In the rugby club the après-game was probably just as
important as the match. The Saturday night sing-song

was an event not to be missed. Tadchester boasted more than its share of pretty girls, many of whom were ready volunteers to help with the food and the bar at the clubhouse. This was an added attraction for the players to linger, and if after a game the clubhouse was actually cleared by midnight, it was unusual.

Although Tadchester was not a first-class rugby club, it was probably not too far off being one. As it was located in a seaside town and offered good hospitality, it attracted touring sides. Many of the best teams in the country, such as Cardiff and Bristol, would come down to play the local side, usually making a weekend of it, playing Tadchester on the Friday and Winchcombe on the Saturday.

Tadchester had its own soccer team, too, which played in the Western League. They had a magnificent stadium, owned by the Council, and each year had the excitement of the preliminary rounds of the FA Cup. They had no actual chance of reaching Wembley, but there was always the hope that they might get far enough to attract some famous side down to Tadchester.

This local team, however, was not composed of locals. They were professionals, some ex-League players. They played football as part of their livelihood, not as part of, or really representing, the town. Many came from as far as fifty or sixty miles away and the end of a game was followed by a quick cup of tea and everybody scurrying off. So unlike the home life of our own dear rugby team.

If rugby was the town's favourite winter sport, cricket was the important exercise for the summer. It had to compete with tennis, swimming, golf and surfing for the No. 1 position, but every hamlet for miles had its own cricket team. In the Tadchester area cricket was more than a game: it was an obsession. There were knockout cups, evening and Sunday leagues, and if you didn't play at least the occasional game of cricket – whatever else you did or didn't do – you didn't belong.

I sometimes kept wicket for the Thudrock Colliery team. Though one of the worst teams in the area, Thudrock probably enjoyed their game more than most. It could have been something to do with their working underground that made them unable to sight the ball properly in daylight on the surface, but they went on cheerfully playing for years without winning a match. As a substitute wicket-keeper, I was absolutely of their standard. The number of byes I let through would sometimes amount to more than the total score of runs made with the bat by our opponents.

Thudrock once put out an open challenge to play any team *underground* for a side stake of £50. They never ever found a challenger. Where they would have played if somebody had taken them up, I have no idea. The biggest open area was the pit bottom which, at its widest, was fifty feet. There would have been boundaries galore from the opposition. However, none of the other teams seemed keen on the idea.

Tadchester Cricket Club played on a pitch at Sanford-on-Sea, a few yards from the sea wall which prevented the low-lying land from being washed away. As it was situated close to the seashore, it could boast a cricket gate as big as many of the county sides. The holidaymakers who invaded the town in the summer would, after a few days, get fed up with making sand castles and waiting for the tide to come in. Looking for some distraction – and there were few others at Sanford-on-Sea – they would climb over the sea wall and watch the cricket matches.

There being nothing like a crowd to attract a crowd, the beach would soon become practically denuded of people. During a match the beach would be populated only by the odd grandma asleep in a deck chair and a few die-hard children, doggedly building intricate sand walls that they knew, definitely, this time would keep the tide at bay.

All would be well, with a couple of thousand people

watching, ball by ball, the fluctuations of the cricket match. Then there would be a scream from one of the abandoned grandmas, wakened by water lapping round her ankles. This would signal a mass exodus by the crowd, who shot off to rescue their towels, picnic baskets, deck chairs, transistors and any other possessions that had not already been swept away by the incoming tide.

The Tadchester Cricket Club worked in close harmony with the tide, and always passed the hat round whilst it was still ebbing, knowing that if they delayed their collection until the tide changed, a take of what might be easily as high as £200 could be as low as £2.

There were few more pleasant sights on a summer's afternoon than that of Kevin Bird, as Tadchester's opening bat. His broad-shouldered hits would send the ball flying over the sea wall time after time. If farming had not been his first love, he could certainly have made a living as a full-time cricket professional.

I watched the cricket as often as I could, but after my first year in Tadchester I never ventured on to the adjoining beach. Interspersed amongst the holiday makers were always a dozen or two of my patients. Seeing their doctor available and unencumbered, it seemed the ideal time to approach him with their latest medical problems. As they were mostly half undressed or in their bathing suits, it was much easier for them to show off their lumps, cuts, rashes, jelly-fish stings and bruises, and saved a long trip to the surgery.

The one thing about the beach was that my patients didn't get lost, as they sometimes did in my surgery.

I had, to some extent, acquired a reputation of being forgetful in the undressing situation. Across from my consulting room was an examination room. If I had someone who needed a full examination I would send him or her off to this room to disrobe while I was seeing the next patient. On a few occasions I became so engrossed in the next cases that I forgot all about my waiting customer. One very embarrassed gentleman whom I had sent to get undressed came back complaining, 'Doctor, there is already a naked lady in the room.'

Twice I had finished my surgery and was off to join my partners for coffee when I heard sobbing in the examination room. On both occasions I found an almost frozen young women who had been sitting in her nether garments for two hours since I had said, 'Go into the examination room, take your clothes off, I'll be with you in a minute.'

My final break with the beach came one sunny afternoon when I had dozed off there in my deck chair. I was wakened by someone surreptitiously coughing in my ear, to find there was a queue of eleven people of different shapes and sizes waiting to consult me . . .

I followed the Tadchester Cricket Club whenever possible and sometimes went on away fixtures with them. I was rewarded on one occasion by being asked to give the toast of 'The Cricket Club' at their annual dinner. I rather fancied myself as an after-dinner speaker and with a responsive audience in the palm of my hand encouraging me, was somewhat inclined to go on and on.

With my stories getting progressively more outrageous, I could have talked all night. I was brought back to earth by the Chairman kicking my ankle and pointing to his watch. Up to this point, having got into my full flow and being a bit full of wine, I had failed to mention the Cricket Club. I made the ultimate gaffe when, having been brought to a halt by the Chairman's kick, I stopped and said, 'Gentlemen, it is with great pleasure that I ask you now to raise your glasses and drink to the health of the Tadchester *Rugby Football Club*.'

They never asked me again.

A quarter of a mile along the coast from the cricket ground

was the famous South Somerset Golf Course. In its heyday it had been one of the main championship courses in the country, but the sea wall wasn't as good as it used to be and didn't protect the land as well as it should have done. During the winter gales the sea would make great inroads through the wall on to the course and the damage to greens and fairways was never quite made up.

There was another problem. Through some ancient bye-law, every householder within a radius of about twenty miles had grazing rights on the common, which included the golf course. As the local population grew, so did the number of people taking up grazing rights, and the common was packed with cattle, horses, goats, sheep and any other quadruped that was able to get some nutrition from the overgrazed grass.

Apart from the hazards of animal droppings on the green, you weren't always safe from the animals themselves: many of the horses were half-wild. Frank Squires once had half his golf bag eaten by a hungry horse as he concentrated on a difficult putt, and one stout lady patient was chased right across the common by two amorous stallions.

When the spring weather came, the golf course became the happy hunting ground of the local 'flashers', who lay behind the bunkers and leapt out, exposing their credentials to whoever might be unfortunate enough to be passing at the time.

Things deteriorated so much that, in time, a round of the South Somerset Golf Course became an endurance test rather than a game of golf. A returning golfer, emerging alive after the completion of a round and being asked how he got on, might well say, 'I was six over par, lost three balls, had two indecent exposures – one of whom I managed to catch with my niblick – one horse bite, one donkey kick, and my feet are covered in sheep droppings.'

The wiser golfers had someone armed with a club and a Polaroid camera riding shotgun for them. The club kept most of the animals away and the camera seemed to be the ideal deterrent for flashers. However great was the desire of these unfortunate and sick men to show their wares, to have them appear in full colour in the Rogues' Gallery at the clubhouse meant that they had entered an area quite outside their personal ambitions. This was one case where it didn't pay to advertise.

CHAPTER 7

Once a week I held a surgery in the branch surgery – a disused garage – for the miners of Thudrock Colliery. These premises were primitive in the extreme, the waiting room and surgery were poorly lit and heated, and the stock of medicines which I had to dispense from consisted mainly for four large bottles filled with different-coloured liquids. On each of the bottles was a printed notice 'Dilute one part of medicine to ten parts of water'.

Somehow these four bottles of medicine were enough to control the health of this small mining community. The medicines were coloured red, green, yellow and black. The black medicine was special and was seen to be special, as written on the outside of the bottle in large letters was 'Special Mixture – Poison'.

I was never quite sure what the medicines contained. I knew the special mixture had some ipecac and a small amount of one of the morphine derivatives in it, but what the others contained is still a mystery. One was reputed to be suitable for coughs, one helped indigestion and one was supposed to be for diarrhoea. However, patients certainly didn't stick to these areas of effectiveness. Often the diarrhoea medicine was demanded for a cough, and the cough medicine for diarrhoea, and so on.

These four bottles of medicine were a tradition, and the miners usually knew which one they required for their particular ailment. A patient would come in and say, 'I think a bit of the green would put me right, doctor.' I never questioned their judgement in these matters, and prescribed accordingly.

One of the more intelligent patients happened to stray into the small room that served as a dispensary and saw me mixing his potion, pouring water to dilute the medicine from one of the stock four bottles.

'Is that all you do, doctor?' he said, 'I could do that.'

'Come on then,' I said, 'mix what you think is right.'

He rejected my offer and grumbled under his breath, 'Yes, I expect you have to have some sort of training.'

The mystique of Medicine had triumphed again.

Always prominent in the medical lore of the hamlet of Thudrock was the black medicine, the Special Mixture. Whereas it could be said that the red, green and yellow bottles were tradition, the black special mix was definitely folklore. I feel sure that it cured as many people and solved as many crises as the mass of antibiotics we have available today.

When an anxious-looking collier called at the surgery and asked, 'Could you come and see my mother, doctor? She is very poorly; I think she'll need a bit of the special,' not only did I know that something was really the matter with Mother, but that I would find a very ill patient.

I also knew that when the patient was given the news that the doctor was on his way and was bringing some of the 'special', she would take heart. However bad she was, she would begin to counter-attack her disease, in much the same way that pioneer American settlers, surrounded by hostile Indians, would buck up when they saw the pennants of the Seventh Cavalry approaching in the distance.

I'd had two years down the mines under the Bevin Scheme at the end of the Second World War, a year and a half of which I had spent at the coal face in a 3 ft 6 in seam with pick and shovel. I learned that miners were marvellous people and that coal-face workers had the same sort of skill and courage as mountaineers.

Twice I was called to Thudrock to go down the mine to attend colliers who had been injured by roof falls. My own mining experiences came back to me as I scrambled along dusty pit roadways with the roof creaking and groaning, threatening to fall.

My first call was to Harry Gilroy, a nineteen-year-old boy whose back had been broken by a fall of rock on one of the pit roadways. In spite of all our care and excellent first aid by the miners on the spot, he finished up paralysed from the waist down. It had been almost impossible to assess his medical condition in the poor light and cramped conditions we had to work in.

About thirty yards of roadway had fallen in, and the boy had been caught at one end of the fall. If he had been in the middle, he would certainly have been killed. The fact that he was on his way to the pit bottom and the fall came up to him from behind rather than in front, meant we were able to get to him direct; otherwise we could have been hours fighting to get through the blocked tunnel.

Whilst I was attending to Harry some colliers had come up from the pit bottom and were adding timbers to protect us from the threatening roof. Each man, as he worked, knew that the roof might come in on us at any moment, but they stuck to their task, erecting metal props and overlapping metal bars, shoring up the roof.

Eventually we managed to get Harry on to a stretcher and start the journey back to the pit bottom. All the time we had been attending him he had been worrying, not about himself but about his pit pony stabled the other side of the fall.

Four of the colliers stayed behind to dig a way through the fall to get the pony out. It was ten hours later that a call was made to Harry in hospital – Black Ben was safe.

Harry Gilroy, now paralysed from the waist down, was engaged to be married. I wondered how this was going to work out.

My other call was to a man with a broken thigh. Working in a 2 ft 6 in seam, a metal prop supporting the roof had flown out and hit him. I had to crawl into the face on my stomach and give him an injection of morphia before we could move him, splint his leg and get him out of the pit. He had been lucky – with proper care he would make a complete recovery.

There was an excellent pithead bath and canteen at Thudrock. The miners could go to the pit in their clean clothes, leave them in their clean lockers, then move across to the other side of the shower room to their dirty lockers and put on their pit clothes.

After they had completed their shift down the mine, they would come back to the baths, put their dirty pit clothes in their dirty lockers, then bath and shower and change into their clean clothes from their clean lockers. After a slap-up subsidised meal in the canteen, they would go home – as clean and well dressed as if they were doing an office job.

There were, however, a few diehards who scorned these modern facilities. They went to the pit half dirty and came home completely dirty.

Not all of Thudrock was fully plumbed, and for some of

these few it still meant heating water in a boiler and bathing in a tin bath in front of the fire. There were still some old-timers who refused to wash their backs at all – they reckoned it would weaken them.

Sometimes a miner would attend the Thudrock surgery outpost in his pit dirt. I tried to discourage this, but the occasional patient slipped through.

One of these was George Marriott. He obviously had some worrying problem, and the coal dirt on his face hid only some of his embarrassment.

'It's like this, doctor,' he said. 'I'm getting married in a month's time, and I have this problem. It's my private parts. It happened in London when I went up for the Cup last year. I had a few too many drinks.'

I could think of no other diagnosis than that of a fairly long-standing venereal disease.

'Let's have a look at you, George,' I said.

George was black all over with coal dust; he could have been signed up for the Black and White Minstrel Show on the spot.

Though I say 'black all over', when he undid his trousers I saw this was not strictly true. Although the rest of him was black, he had scrubbed clean the most male part of his anatomy so that it stood out as a shining white pillar on a black background.

'Now, George,' I said, 'what is the trouble? Have you a discharge or a sore anywhere?'

'Oh, no,' said George, 'nothing like that. When I was five parts gone in London, me mates dragged me into a tattooist, and look what they did to me!'

I had great difficulty in stopping myself laughing.

There was the sheepish, embarrassed, coal-black George, with his spotless white member protruding. On it, in an almost copperplate hand, was tattooed *God Bless the Queen*. I thought I had seen tattoos on every part of the body, but this was a new one for me.

Trying to look and sound as serious as I could, I said

'Yes, George. I see you have a problem. I will send you to a skin specialist. Sometimes they can remove tattoos. If not, he may be able to change the writing into a blue line – and it will look like a coal scar.'

The tears of gratitude from George made white lines down his black face.

The four partners – Steve, Jack, Henry and I, always met for coffee each morning. It was the time to discuss problems, hand cases on, and to produce some funny story to lighten the day.

Steve, my senior partner, was a marvellous audience. He usually burst out laughing before I had completed my stories, and had a fund of improbable stories of his own which usually capped whatever tale I might produce – true or otherwise. I could hardly wait to tell them of my 'God Bless the Queen' experience.

The next morning, when I described my encounter with George, Henry and Jack roared with laughter. Steve smiled rather than laughed, and said 'Once I had a similar case. A young man came to the surgery with a boil in his groin. I noticed, during my examination, that he had the letters LDO tattooed on his penis. The boil needed poulticing, so I sent him out to the nurse to have the poultice applied, and arranged for him to come for dressings.

'We had a particularly attractive nurse at that time – Audrey Deryton. She came back to me at the end of the surgery, not knowing whether to laugh or die of embarrassment.

' "Oh, doctor," she said, "did you see where that man had LLANDUDNO tattooed?" '

We collapsed, laughing – Steve had won again.

I welcomed Albert Scotherm when he retired and came to live in Tadchester. He had been a coal miner in Yorkshire and was one of those wise old men like Bob Barker whom I could sit and listen to for hours.

He was an old scallywag, and had been a well-known south Yorkshire local councillor as well as a coal miner. He had not lost his broad Yorkshire dialect. He would say: 'It was like this Bob, lad. Council meetings were getting a bit dreary. They just droned on doing nowt. So one day I took a revolver in t'council chamber. When t'Town Clerk were in the middle of some speech about rehousing, I fired t'revolver under t'table. It were only a blank, but it gave out a reet good bang. It really shook 'em all up, but it were a bad joke. Town Clerk collapsed wi' a heart attack, had six weeks in hospital, and I was banned from all t'council meetings for a month.'

Albert had gone down the pit at the age of fourteen to work on the haulage. By going to night school and day-release courses at the university, he had reached the position of colliery manager by the time he retired. What was more important to me than Albert's anecdotes was that he had been a close friend of my father's. I had lost my father when I was very young, and my memories of him were blurred. Albert could fill in the gaps in my knowledge about him.

He and my father had attended Sheffield University on day-release courses from the pit when they were both working underground as electrical engineers. They stuck at their course and both eventually passed their degree papers in mining engineering.

'We were pleased as Punch,' said Albert, 'but then Sheffield University wrote to us saying that they could not award the degrees as neither of us had matriculated. As we'd both left school at fourteen this weren't surprising. If we wanted our degree, they said, we'd have to do us matriculation. That were enough for me,' said Albert. 'I gave it up, but not your Dad. He were like a terrier, he stuck at it.'

My father apparently, after a hard day's work down below, went back to his miner's cottage in the evening and started the tedious task of taking his matriculation by

85

correspondence course. This included French – and if his Yorkshire accent was anything like Albert's, this must have been akin to climbing Everest. Amid all his studies he still took time off to work on his various inventions – my mother still draws a small royalty from some automatic coal-tub braking system he invented. Somehow he got through his matriculation only to be told by the university that they now required him to take his inter BSc examination before they would award his degree. Undeterred, he went back to his cottage kitchen, setting up his own apparatus for his physics and chemistry experiments.

I had found bits and pieces of this experimental apparatus in a drawer at home. There was a piece of glass from an old chandelier which he used as a prism, and a gold-leaf electroscope that he had manufactured himself. He passed his inter BSc with a credit in physics, only to be told by the university that all he was now required to do for his degree was – to sit the final papers again.

This was too much, even for my father. In the meantime he had been awarded his AMIEE, and he decided to call it a day with universities. There was some poetic justice for him in that some years later, when he was an internationally known engineer, Liverpool University honoured him with the degree of Master of Engineering, *honoris causa*.

Father's university setback seemed to spur him on. At the age of twenty-five he grew a moustache to make him look older and managed to get appointed as the chief electrical engineer to the Kent coalfield, and became in his spare time the Chairman of Deal Rowing Club. For many this would have been enough, but my father hated coal mines. After a few years he gave it all up and became the personal assistant to an eccentric American millionaire.

Giving up a safe job (he was married by then) must have been a tremendous risk. The idea was that he and the millionaire would work together on inventions. Either the inventions were not successful or the partnership didn't work out, for after a year my father found himself out of work. He eventually managed to get a job with the Central Electricity Board somewhere in the north.

From then on he never looked back. He rose steadily through the ranks of the electricity supply industry, finishing up as member for operations and personnel of the Central Electricity Generating Board which controlled the entire production of electricity in England and Wales. On the way up, he collected a CBE.

Outside his work he was involved in all sorts of activities. He founded a club of engineers called the Nasmyth Club, named after one of his heroes – James Nasmyth, the inventor of the steam hammer. This was a dining-club of engineers who would invite celebrities from outside the engineering field to dine with them and be interrogated about their work and way of life. Their guests included a poet, a medium, and Shipton the Arctic explorer. They invited H. G. Wells to be a guest but the great man reversed their invitation and acted as host to the club at a birthday dinner at his home.

In addition to all this, my father was collecting all sorts of awards for learned papers, including the John Hopkinson award and the Williams Medal as well as various American honours. He became the first English-speaking president of CIGRE, which is an international organisation for countries that have grid systems of electricity. He was host to three thousand delegates of that organisation at a conference reception at the Palace of Versailles.

He was a restless ambitious man and after a time felt he had explored the electricity industry, so he moved to private industry and even greater success. He was a talented writer and broadcaster; some of his short stories were broadcast in the intervals during celebrity concerts. He was a first-class black-and-white artist – I still have some of his drawings – as well as being an accomplished pianist.

But, above all, he was a kind and sensitive man who apparently valued his relationships with people more than he did any of his achievements.

Albert said that my father's office was like a psychiatrist's waiting room, with people going in for advice not about engineering and their jobs – but about their despairs, depressions, family and economic troubles. I realised that I would never be as brilliant as he was, nor as well remembered.

He didn't even waste a spell in hospital. In the next bed was a blind and deaf airman called Wally Thomas and my father, being my father, was frustrated at not being able to communicate with him. After his discharge from hospital he set to and invented a blind-deaf aid. It enabled people who did not know the hand language by which you can communicate with the blind-deaf, to tap out on a normal typewriter keyboard what they wanted to say. The blind-deaf would pick up the typed transcript message on Braille studs attached to the machine. The Carnegie Trust eventually paid for the final development and production of this aid.

'Well,' said Albert one day as he was recounting my father's achievements, 'you may bring lots of new babies into the world, Bob lad – but I'll bet you'll never give birth to new inventions like your Dad did.'

CHAPTER 8

I found in Tadchester that I had to compete with my medical skills against the local folk medicine and old wives' tales that were so dear to the hearts of the locals.

Women coming to my ante-natal clinic were asked routinely if they were having any trouble with their bowels. Most would say, 'No, doctor. I go about five or six times a day.'

What they meant was that this was quite the normal output for any woman pregnant in Tadchester. It was a firmly rooted tradition that if the pregnant young mum was dosed often enough with large quantities of liquid paraffin it would grease the baby and help towards a smooth and easy delivery. However much I protested against this procedure and enlarged on its dangers, I knew that as soon as the young woman got home grandma would say, 'Don't you take any notice of that young man; he's barely out of medical school. Here, have another spoonful. I've mixed in a bit of orange squash to make it taste better.'

Any skin blemish on a newborn baby, never mind a birth-mark proper, was immediately related to something that had happened in pregnancy. A mouse shape was supposed to mean that the mother had been frightened by a mouse. Any sort of semi-circle was identified as a horse-shoe and meant the mother had been frightened by a horse. I thought they would be caught out when I delivered a baby with a tuft of hair over its right buttock, but the mother, after much deliberation, came out with an answer. She remembered being bumped into by a Shet-land pony.

Signs in pregnancy, I was told, would predict charac-teristics of the coming baby. If the mother had indigestion it meant that the baby was going to be born with a lot of hair. If the baby kicked a lot then it was definitely going to be a boy. In Tadchester, however, if the expectant mother wanted definite sexing of her coming child, she would visit Granny Watson in her caravan, and for the sum of one shilling she would get her answer.

Granny would dangle the mother's wedding ring on a piece of cotton over the mother's navel. If it swung to and fro, it was going to be a boy; if it swung round and round, it was going to be a girl. Many amateurs tried to emulate Granny Watson, but she was accredited with having the true sensitivity. She must have had a high success rate because she was never short of customers.

The only infallible sexer I knew was Henry Johnson. When he was asked by a mother-to-be 'Is it going to be a boy or a girl, doctor?' he would put his hand on her stomach and then make an instant diagnosis, saying positively either, 'This is going to be a boy,' or, 'This is going to be a girl.' He would then make a show of taking out his diary to write down his prediction.

What the mother didn't know was that what he wrote in his diary was the exact opposite to the prediction he had made to her. When the baby was finally delivered, if what he had originally predicted was true, it was all congratulations. If, however, it was the exact opposite from his prediction, he would look puzzled, take out his diary, then with a smiling face would say, 'No, I *am* right – look, I wrote it down in my diary when you asked me.'

I am sure he did a lot of irreparable psychological harm to a lot of young mothers, leaving them confused and worried about their memory, but nobody ever doubted Henry and he always got away with it.

One of my biggest battles conducted in the ante-natal clinic was against the amount of weight that some of the young mothers put on. There was a Tadchester granny's theory – 'The bigger the mother, the bigger the baby.' Some of these poor young women must have had a sympathy with the poor Hungarian geese who are literally stuffed alive to make *pâté de foie gras*. I could not convince them that having a big mother didn't make a big baby, that all it did was to make labour and delivery more difficult and cumbersome.

Folklore even crept into breast-feeding. Hardly any Tadchester feeding mother would eat oranges: it was felt that they curdled the milk.

More than one person believed that if an expectant mother put sticking plaster over her navel it would kill the baby, and a cough during pregnancy was always attributed to the baby's foot tickling the mother's windpipe.

Unwanted pregnancies in Tadchester were about on a par with most other places. The standard abortifacients appeared to be mainly castor oil and gin – they were rarely successful.

I discovered a more original method when a young couple, girl and boy-friend, came in together. They both complained that they had trouble with their right feet. They both had a right foot-drop which meant they were unable to lift the top of their foot up towards the knee. This was a sign of some neurological trouble, and the fact that both should have absolutely identical symptoms seemed extremely strange. I had to send them off to be completely investigated by a neurologist. The results of the investigations were that they were both suffering from lead poisoning. Happily, said the specialist's report, once the source of lead was tracked down and stopped, the nerve debility in their legs should recover.

It took some probing and prying to find their lead source, but eventually the girl confessed that she was pregnant, and that she had bought some pills to try and get rid of the pregnancy. To make sure that they weren't harmful to her, she had insisted that her boy-friend take at least the same quantity as she did. Analysis showed that the pills had a fairly high lead content – and this was the cause of the trouble in both of them. Once the pills were stopped, their legs did recover. The baby was quite unaffected and arrived at the exact time and date predicted.

A local cure for mumps in Tadchester was to rub the swellings with a snail. Always the lumps went away afterwards. That they also always went away without rubbing them with a snail didn't seem to make any difference to the treatment. Tadchester people wore copper bracelets to ward off rheumatism, but the *Tadchester Guardian* of 1805 went one better when it announced that a new cure for the same condition had been found – to bury yourself up to the neck in the churchyard for two hours. I wish this treatment was prescribable on the National Health Service. I could think of several patients I could recommend it to – and not just to cure their rheumatism.

One of my old ladies kept a magnet at the side of her bed to keep rheumatism away, and another used to turn her slippers over at night to stop the cramps. Another practical cure for the cramps was two ounces of sulphur on a plate under the bed.

There were two schools of thought for the treatment of lumbago. One believed that a belt of leather next to the skin was the most effective treatment, whilst another preferred a violin string tied round the waist. I wondered if this latter remedy was the precursor of the G-string – perhaps some old-time stripper had seized up just before her performance and decided that the show must go on . . .

When examining patients in their beds at home, I was always coming across odd potatoes between the sheets and sometimes a pocket magnet or piece of camphor in the pyjama pocket. For warts there was a battery of recommended treatments, but most people waited until the fair came for the summer carnival, when the gypsy fortune-teller would charm the warts away. Spiders' webs were put on cuts: these did help the blood to clot, but were also likely to infect the wound with a hefty dose of bacteria.

I once went out to an isolated farm to find the farmer with an infected, almost gangrenous, leg covered with a dressing of mouldy bread.

'What on earth have you put that stuff on his leg for?' I asked.

'Oh doctor,' said the farmer's wife, 'we always keep a loaf of mouldy rye bread in the ceiling rafter for infected cuts.'

'These old-wives' tales will be the death of all of you,' I said. I was furious.

I had to admit the farmer to hospital, where he was found to be diabetic. He had a long spell on both insulin and penicillin before we were able to get his leg into good enough shape for him to go back to his farm.

Talking to Steve about this patient one morning at coffee, I said, 'When will these people ever learn? Fancy putting mouldy bread on infected cuts.'

Steve said, 'Don't you be too hasty with them, Bob. Mouldy bread has cured more infected cuts than it has let go bad. These people discovered penicillin long before Sir Alexander Fleming did. The mould on that bread is mainly penicillin mould: it's been used in this way for some hundreds of years. And it's not any old mouldy bread; it's good rye bread, hung up in the rafters where it's well ventilated.'

He laughed. 'I will agree with you, it's a bit out of date now, but belief in the treatment plus a bit of medication goes a long way towards a cure.'

Steve's words were only too well illustrated by Harry Bagshaw. Harry was a labourer at the brick works on the Up-the-Hill side of the river. He came to my surgery one evening straight from work and covered in brick dust.

'I think I've ruptured myself, doctor,' he said. 'Could you fix me up?'

His diagnosis was correct. He had a double rupture, a large round swelling in each groin.

'I'm afraid it's a hospital job for you, Harry,' I said. 'I'll get you an appointment to see Mr Johnson at the hospital. You need an operation to put this right.'

'No,' said Harry. 'I can't be off work. I've got eight kids to feed. I just want a truss like some of my mates have.'

He wouldn't be persuaded to come into hospital, so I reluctantly wrote out a prescription for him for a double inguinal truss. This is a strap-like arrangement that belts round the waist and pulls up pads in both groins to support the hernias.

I didn't see Harry for two years. One evening he turned up at the surgery, again in his brick dust.

'I'd like another truss please, doctor,' he said. 'What with all the dirt and sweat at work, this one has got a bit worn.'

I raised the question of an operation again, but once more Harry declined.

94

'I've had no trouble at all since I've had this truss, doctor.'

'Well, let's have a look at you.'

Harry reluctantly slid his trousers down. I found that he now had a *huge* swelling in each groin – much worse than when I had last seen him.

'That truss isn't doing much,' I said. 'These hernias are much worse. Bring your truss in to me tomorrow and let me have a look at it.'

'I'm *wearing* it,' said Harry. 'I never take it off.'

He took off his shirt and there, strapped round his chest, was his truss – with the pads that should have been support-ing his groins firmly ensconced under each arm. I could hardly believe it, but I saw Harry's logic. They looked like braces, so he wore them as braces.

He still would not agree to go for operation, so I ordered him a new truss, made him bring it to the surgery and showed him how to put it on. He was to report back after wearing it for a fortnight. He duly reported after two weeks and I asked, 'How are you getting on now, Harry?'

'I expect things are better in one way,' said Harry, 'but it were much more comfortable when I wore 'em round my shoulders.'

I knew that with so many of my patients like Harry I would always be fighting an uphill battle.

I never minded my casualty duties at Tadchester Hospital. We worked a rota system, sharing the duties between five of us. The only time it became a bit onerous was in the summer. With the population swollen by some thousands, you tended to work very hard all the time you were on call for casualty.

There was no resident doctor at Tadchester Hospital, which had sixty beds and came under the loose category of a cottage hospital. Apart from the work done in the hospital by our practice, various consultants from Winch-combe Hospital held out-patient clinics there, and one of the Winchcombe surgeons had two major surgical operating sessions each week.

Although the occasional regular patient of mine would get up to casualty to buttonhole me about some particular worry, casualty was mainly casualty: instead of having to listen so much to people, I would be doing practical work with my hands.

Casualty work was extremely varied. I gave some anaesthetics for Henry when he had fractures to reduce or abscesses to open and explore. There was a great deal of stitching up of cuts to do, and I prided myself on my needlework, taking a great deal of time and trouble to produce a neat job. The time I took used to make the casualty sister very restless. She would look over my shoulder impatiently and say, 'Are you hoping that they are going to hang this in the Tate, doctor?'

One casualty seemed very familiar. She was – it was Gladys, our senior receptionist.

'What are you doing here?' I asked.

'I've been trying to attract somebody's attention in the surgery all week,' said Gladys (and I must say that I had been vaguely conscious of Gladys limping around a bit). 'If I walked in with an arrow sticking through my head, all I would be asked would be "How many patients are booked in today?" so I've come here for some attention.'

I had a look at Gladys's leg. She had an extensive burn down its whole length. I couldn't imagine how she had managed to keep going; it must have been very painful. I got the staff nurse to dress it and told Gladys she would have to have a week off from work.

'Rubbish!' said Gladys. 'It's much better. If one of you had had a look at it a week ago it would probably have been completely cured by now!'

There was no doubt that we neglected medically the people with whom we were in immediate contact. Patsy Johnson, Henry's wife, once got so fed up with trying to get him to take some notice of a rash she had on her arm, that in the end she made a surgery appointment to see her husband, and sat in the waiting-room with the rest of the patients, in her hat and coat. Even the phlegmatic Henry, after ringing for the next patient, was taken somewhat aback when his wife stormed in, saying, 'Now about this arm I've been asking you to look at for weeks . . .'

I was an expert at getting foreign bodies out of ears and noses, but not so expert about getting them out of other places. One afternoon I had a male patient arrive at casualty, limping and in obvious pain. He insisted that he saw me in a cubicle on my own, away from the nurse.

'It's very embarrassing, doctor,' he whispered. 'I slipped and sat on this glue pot and it stuck in my back passage.'

I thought how unfortunate the poor chap had been and was surprised that he wasn't more shocked. It didn't occur to me at the time that he couldn't have had his trousers on when this catastrophe happened. I made a painful and unsuccessful attempt to remove it, then called in Henry. With some difficulty he removed the pot while I gave the patient an anaesthetic.

'Have you ever seen anything like that before?' I asked Henry. 'The chances of its happening must be infinitesimal.'

Henry roared, 'Good God, lad, you didn't believe him, did you? That's the way he had his fun. He is, for want of a better term, a sexual deviant.'

With my innocence shattered I was at least in some way prepared a few months later when a smartly dressed young man appeared in casualty and asked to see me privately. I showed him into a cubicle. His dress was immaculate, he was relaxed and when I asked about his particular problem, he replied nonchalantly, 'I've got a cucumber stuck, doctor, I would be grateful if you would yank it out.'

Nonplussed and grasping for some words to answer his nonchalance, I asked, 'Is it peeled?'

The reply was scornful in the extreme. 'Of *course* it's peeled.'

I was able to manage this particular operation without calling for help and marvelled at the eccentricities and strange private pastimes of my fellow men.

One part of casualty duty I did not enjoy. This was dealing with people who had tried to take their lives as the answer to their problems, most commonly through an overdose of drugs. We had to put them through the degrading process of being held down while a tube was forced down the throat into the stomach and the stomach contents washed out. During my time in Tadchester, the number of attempted suicides steadily increased year by year until it became the commonest single cause for admission to the medical ward.

The casualty staff hated dealing with these overdoses as I did. 'These awful physical fights to get stomach tubes down really degrade us, doctor,' the staff nurse said.

We kept the would-be suicides in at least overnight. They were seen the next day by the psychiatrist who tried to explore the problem that had led to their attempting to take their lives. A few would agree to go into his hospital and have themselves sorted out, but most packed themselves off back home – and back to their problems – as soon as they could.

I talked to the psychiatrist, Dr Lester, who was based at a large hospital near Winchcombe. I asked if there was any answer to this increasing problem of attempted suicide, and what it was all about.

He said that of every hundred patients whom he saw who had attempted to take their lives (and he preferred the term 'self-poisoning' to 'attempted suicide') ten had some long-standing type of depressive illness, and fifteen had some sort of mental abnormality. Of the remaining seventy-five, the only common factor was that sixty-five per cent of them either knew someone closely who had tried the same thing, or had in fact attempted to do it themselves before. He thought that the whole problem was a social rather than a medical one.

'For example,' he said, 'if you have a large resident community such as a factory hostel or a nurses' home, and one girl attempts self-poisoning, in the next few months several more will have a go. It's almost as if it were infectious. It's the same with local communities. The highest attempted-self-poisoning rate is in a rural area of Wales.

'The answer lies to some extent in how we house people, where communities are situated, what access they have to recreation and distractions away from their particular problems. The break-up and present-day looseness of family ties isn't any help. There are no longer the great family structures that people could fall back on for support and help.'

I discussed the problem with Steve. He agreed with most of Dr Letter's views.

'If you notice, Bob, that of our young mothers in Tadchester who become depressed after childbirth, ninety per cent of them are not natives of the town. They haven't grans and mums and aunts to help them through this very important period of their lives.'

'Is there an answer?' I asked.

'I believe there is a very simple answer to everything,' said Steve. 'I believe there is a formula. If people could form the habit of making a conscious effort to do one unselfish act a day, most of the problems of everyday life would disappear. The simpler any remedy is, generally the more effective it is.'

Steve was the most unselfish and self-contained man I ever met. If most of us were ever able to reach his sort of standards, I would agree there would be few problems of any sort.

CHAPTER 9

There was an emergency call to Sanford-on-Sea holiday camp. By the time I arrived it was too late to do anything.

A child had been found drowning in the small paddling pool in the middle of the camp. She had been pulled out of the water and a holidaymaker, a first-aider, had taken over the situation and had given her mouth-to-mouth resuscitation. She was quite dead when I arrived.

It was only at the post-mortem that the full extent of the tragedy was revealed. The child had not died of drowning, but of suffocation from vomit in the back of her throat – blown into her lungs by the first-aider. If she had just been laid on her face, and nobody had tried to revive her, she might well have lived.

There were two lots of people to console: the grief-stricken parents and, possibly even more so, the poor first-aider. He had done what he had been trained to do, what he had been told always should be done, and had probably done it extremely efficiently within the limits of his training.

Subsequently I had a continuous running battle with the senior first-aid administrators. It was my view that mouth-to-mouth resuscitation was not always the best method of reviving people, particularly in cases of drowning.

The one procedure that all first-aiders know, or think they know, is mouth-to-mouth resuscitation. They are all dying to have a go at it. They have been trained on resuscitation Annies (lifelike rubber facsimiles of a young girl). They have to blow into rubber Annie's mouth and watch her chest expand. There are various other things to be done – look into her mouth, pinch her nose and position her head properly. Thousands of first-aiders all over the country become very proficient at using Annie. For many, alas, this is as far as the proficiency goes. There is a great deal of difference between a rubber dummy and a human being.

Before attempting to give mouth-to-mouth resuscitation, you have first to be skilled enough to be able to determine whether the patient has actually stopped breathing or not. A doctor, with his skill and his instruments, finds it difficult enough. Often only a slight change in the position of the patient's head is enough to restart breathing.

It has always been one of my private nightmares that one day I could be in a situation where I had some difficulty in breathing. Just when I was beginning to get my breath back, I would be pounced on by a great big first-aider and I would be too weak to prevent him from clamping his mouth on mine and trying to blow me up.

The biggest hazard in mouth-to-mouth resuscitation is something blocking the airways. However much you look into the mouth (and I am sure our first-aider *had* looked into the little girl's mouth) you cannot see round the back of the pharynx unless you have a special instrument (a laryngoscope). There doesn't have to be much material lurking round this corner. It could be some thick mucus, a bit of seaweed, or as in the little girl's case, some vomit. One steady blow into a debilitated patient could put this material straight into his lungs and possibly kill him. I am never sure when I read reports of people being saved by mouth-to-mouth resuscitation whether they recovered because of it or in spite of it.

For the average first-aider the chances are that perhaps only once in a lifetime will he be called on to give artificial respiration. I can never see how he can be expected to give it properly and effectively, including all the medical assessments that have to be made before starting the procedure. How much simpler to lay the patient on his face with the mouth clear and unobstructed and get air into the chest by pressing rhythmically on the back. A less efficient method, but so much safer.

I wonder if the people who outlined first-aid treatment had the same sort of practical experience as I had as a GP in a coastal holiday town where drowning and collapsing cases were only too frequent. Were their views based on their own experience or were they just sticking to their first-aid book? Every procedure must be under constant review.

For years the treatment of adder bite in this country was to rush the patient to hospital and give him some anti-venom. Apart from tying a ligature round bitten limbs, this was the standard treatment.

Then there came a time when the British Red Cross Society asked the School of Hygiene and Tropical Medicine to investigate the treatment of snake bite in Britain. Their findings were that the only available anti-venom at that time was (a) no use at all against adder bites; it was made in South America and it was therapeutic against one specific type of South American snake only; (b) because the anti-venom was made from horse serum, to which sensitive people can react fatally, the anti-venom injections were not only useless against the snake bite but more dangerous than the bite itself. It is only recently that an effective anti-venom has become available.

I fought a lone battle over my views on mouth-to-mouth resuscitation. I have the greatest respect for the first-aid organisations, and hope that perhaps one day they will have another look at all resuscitation procedures.

The girls in my Forward Medical Aid Unit were a mixture of Red Cross and St John's. They were a marvellous lot and all did stout work at the holiday camps and beaches at Tadchester during the summer. They all learnt mouth-to-mouth resuscitation, or anyway they learnt to blow up rubber Annie. But we discussed resuscitation as a whole: they would think before they tried any procedure; they would assess the whole situation of a collapsed, unconscious or drowning patient and look to the best way of revival. They did not, as so many appear to do, say to themselves, 'At last I've found somebody who's stopped breathing; here's my chance to see if I can blow him up.'

Alas, I had no control over visiting first-aiders and, although I managed to stop one giving mouth-to-mouth resuscitation to a boy who was having an epileptic fit, I was unable to stop another enthusiast who insisted on continuing to blow for more than two hours into someone who was dead from a broken neck.

One morning over coffee with my partners, I asked the phlegmatic Henry for his views on first-aiders giving mouth-to-mouth resuscitation.

'Lot of bloody rubbish,' said Henry. 'Just take their teeth out, lay them down on their stomachs, and give them a thump on the back.'

Henry, being Henry, was somehow always successful in any procedure he tried for whatever purpose. It always seemed to work for him, or anyway he got away with it. I thought his suggested resuscitation procedures were probably as good as any.

I think our lighter moments, when we shared our morning coffee, were of tremendous benefit to us. We could discuss our worries and laugh them off. Life can be so cruel, so tragic and so unfair. I believe it is only by trying to laugh at our troubles that we manage to survive them. However, some people seem to have a much greater share of misfortune than others – and some troubles are beyond laughter.

Amongst my patients there were many who complained of misfortune and the way life had treated them harshly, and how unfair it all was. Those, however, who really had had a raw deal from life – whose misfortunes were of a magnitude that one questioned whether there was any justice anywhere – did not seem to complain in the same way. They accepted their burdens as part of their lot and carried on with tremendous courage the task of living.

One such family were the Whites. They lived out in the country, Up-the-Hill, about two miles from the main residential area, in a tied cottage, Mr White working as a farm labourer. There were six normal, happy and healthy children. They were a self-contained family and did not ask for much from anybody, and were as successful at the level they lived as anybody could be. They rarely visited the surgery so I did not get to know them until the youngest son (Nigel) was brought to me. He 'wasn't himself': he was floppy and listless and obviously had something generally wrong with him which had been insidious in its onset. By the time I saw him he had difficulty getting about; he felt listless, lethargic, and was a bit withdrawn.

I sent him to the children's specialist at Winchcombe who, in turn, sent him to Great Ormond Street Children's Hospital in London.

He came back with a diagnosis of some strange disease that I had never heard of and which meant that his nervous system would gradually break down, that he would become progressively weaker, and would be unlikely to survive more than a couple of years.

Nigel looked fit and healthy apart from the fact that he couldn't hold his head up and his limbs drooped. He was a large eight-year-old and, as his condition got worse, his mother had to carry him around as if he were a baby. There were several attempts at treatment of his condition but he didn't respond. The poor lad barely survived the two years predicted as the maximum he could live.

The family took his death well – if any death can be taken well. It had been obvious that it was coming and they had prepared themselves for it, although this did not lessen the awful loss when it came.

I feel that people who are close to the land and are involved in the rearing of livestock are better equipped to deal with the life/death situation. The animals they rear have to be sent off to be killed; they see animals die, and thus accept that death is inseparable from living.

It was only six months after Nigel's death that I was called to see his ten-year-old sister, Dorothy. I made a confident diagnosis of appendicitis (she had had abdominal pain and sickness) and sent her to hospital. I gave her the anaesthetic while Henry operated, and expected that it would be a simple operation, and that she would be home in a matter of about a week.

When Henry opened her abdomen we found, to our horror, that her pain was not from the appendix but from a widespread cancer of one of her ovaries. I did not even know it was possible for children to have this condition.

Henry did his best, without offering any hope, and I broke the news to the parents as gently as I could. For eighteen months we lived in a nightmare, watching with the parents their second child fade and eventually die.

Towards the end of her illness Dorothy would see no one apart from her family and myself. She would scream filthy abuse at the vicar when he called, but would accept me because to some extent I could relieve her fears and pains.

For the second time the family had to face a terrible loss and, not least, heavy funeral expenses. The wage of a farm labourer at that time was little above subsistence level. All the family rallied round and helped out with the expenses. The fact that they were a large family helped them survive this second, awful ordeal. They *did* survive it, but for a time they were very bewildered, and for some months Mrs White was apprehensive about any of her children becoming ill. She would bring them to the surgery for the slightest cough, cold, ache or pain. The odds for either of those two conditions arising in any family were so small that you could almost eliminate the possibility. That the odds were defeated twice left me with an emptiness that I could not describe.

The Whites were a good-living family – solid, respectable, hard-working people. Why should they have had to bear all this? I could think of many people who merited ill fortune: I could see no reason why this particular family deserved any ill fortune at all.

A year later Mrs White, who was almost past child-bearing age, gave birth to a baby girl. The child became the spoiled darling of the whole family, demanded everybody's attention and managed to help erase some of the memories of the losses of the previous two years. Somehow it seemed that Nature – or whatever – had thought that they had suffered enough and did its best to balance their loss and sufferings.

Dealing with situations such as those in the White family made me take a long, hard look at myself as a general practitioner. It was too easy with so many people dependent on me to perhaps unconsciously develop inflated ideas about myself as a doctor – that I had to solve most people's problems, that I was important.

The Whites brought home to me the fact that there were whole areas of medicine where I just acted as a signpost to my more specialised colleagues, that any hope of cure lay with them alone; that all I could do was to pass patients on to them and be available to act as a comforter if necessary.

Daphne Wallcott was an attractive blonde-haired nineteen-year-old, and a keen tennis player. She worked in the bank where I had my account and always waved to me when I went in.

When she came to see me in the surgery she was all apologies. Sorry to come about nothing . . . probably just a strain . . .

'Sit down, Daphne,' I said, 'and let me decide what is wrong. Just take your time and tell me what's troubling you.'

Daphne complained about a lot of little things – her

eyes, and odd muscle troubles. She said, 'I sound silly, telling you all these things. I feel perfectly well. I can manage my work. The only thing is, I'm all wrong with my tennis. I don't know what it is. Do you think I'm just run down? I eat well and sleep well. Mother thinks it's just nerves, but there's nothing I feel nervous about.'

I examined Daphne and found that she had some definite neurological symptoms. Various things didn't work quite as they should and some of her muscle reflexes weren't equal.

'Well, Daphne,' I said, 'Mother is right in one way. Your nerves are upset but not in the way she means. Something has upset them, and I mean by that some of the nerve fibres in your body. I don't know what is causing it so we shall have to send you to a neurologist, who specialises in these matters.'

'What about my tennis?' Daphne asked. 'We have the club championship in a fortnight.'

I said, 'Well you mustn't play if you feel at all unwell or if your muscles don't work quite as they should. I'll make an appointment for you to see the neurologist. Report back to me a week after you have seen him. If in the meantime there are any other symptoms, come and see me. It's likely that all these little things you complain of will get better on their own but I mustn't take any chances with our potential Wimbledon champion; that's why I am making this appointment.'

Daphne got much better over the next two weeks and was well enough to win the Tadchester Ladies' Tennis Championship. By the time she saw the neurologist she hardly had any symptoms at all.

The letter from the neurologist was as I thought it would be. He wrote, 'This young lady shows definite signs of early disseminated sclerosis. She appears to be getting better, so for the present I would do nothing about it. If her condition should change, I should be pleased to see her again. I have told her that part of her nervous system has become inflamed, that it appears to be getting better, that if she is at all worried about herself to come and see you.'

I took the letter to Steve, my senior partner. He read it thoughtfully, then looked over his half-rimmed glasses and said, 'What are you going to say to her?'

'Well,' I replied, 'just the same as the specialist, that she has had an inflammation of a part of the nervous system and that it appears to be getting better.'

'Good,' said Steve. 'Over the years I have acquired great doubts as to whether there is a specific disease of disseminated sclerosis. Broadly it just means that a patient's nervous system, for no reason that we know of, has started to break down. The characteristic of this so-called disease is that it undergoes remissions spontaneously. For no known reason it disappears in much the same way as it starts. More often than not, the patients get completely better. There are, of course, some who don't and have a progressive deterioration.

'If you tie a label to people they consciously or unconsciously try to behave according to the description on the label. If you tell Daphne she has disseminated sclerosis, then always at the back of her mind there'll be the thought that she has a progressive disease. I believe these thoughts at the back of the mind are destructive, that they themselves help to actuate the disease.

'We come back to the vexed problem of what to tell patients, and when. I don't think you can generalise. I think you have to consider every patient individually and decide what you say to them after you have considered their particular situation alone. Sometimes I think we cripple people by telling them they have a certain disease. We do this, not always having the complete facts and thus the complete right to tell them.

'With the particular condition that Daphne has, the neurologist is right. She has some inflamed nerves that are getting better. That we should tie the label "disseminated sclerosis" on these symptoms is, to my personal belief, wrong.

'There are no true statistics about this particular disease, mainly because general practitioners are poor at keeping records. If someone disappears after being diagnosed, they don't enter the statistics, and the most common reason for their not reappearing is that they continue to be perfectly well. Unfortunately we base most of our records on people who don't do so well.'

He pointed to his file of patients' records. 'In there, Bob,' he said, 'I could find you a couple of dozen patients who have been diagnosed as having disseminated sclerosis. That's as far as the disease ever went with them. They've never known they were supposed to have had it, and they have gone on in perfectly good health for ten, twenty, thirty years, with no history of trouble. I wonder how they would have fared if I had told them the initial diagnosis. I may be wrong, but I doubt if they would have done as well. At the very least they would have always had to carry an extra worry.'

In my early years in general practice I leant heavily on Steve for his wisdom and advice. He was able to cover areas of patients' treatment and management that did not appear in textbooks. I was really an apprentice to a craftsman. Just over a century ago this was the way in which most doctors were trained. You could only properly learn your craft by working with and under a master craftsman.

When Daphne came to see me I confirmed what the neurologist had told her – that she had some inflamed nerves. When I saw her a month later, she was quite free of symptoms. Twenty-five years later, when she was looking forward to the birth of her first grandchild, she did not know that two and a half decades and eight tennis championships earlier she had been diagnosed as suffering from disseminated sclerosis.

CHAPTER 10

I was an active member of the Tadchester Round Table, a sort of junior Rotary Club. Candidates have to be under forty years of age to join, and the Table members are limited to one representative from each of the professions. This meant that we could have one doctor, one solicitor, one butcher and one school teacher, etc. as members.

We kept the rules fairly elastic and if there was more than one of any particular calling keen to join, we would stretch them so that there could be, for example, a general practitioner and an anaesthetist, a headmaster and a form master.

Tadchester Round Table met twice a month in a room

at the Tadchester Arms where they had a dinner, conducted their business, and usually had a guest speaker. They were a lively lot and were heavily involved in activities outside their meetings. These consisted mainly of various types of community service. They would arrange outings for such groups as the blind, mentally handicapped children, and old age pensioners. The rest of the time was taken up in charity fund raising. They took a major part in arranging Tadchester Carnival, as well as participating in it. They also staged a donkey derby during Carnival week. Their other money-raising activities were through such things as raffles, dances and motor rallies.

Tadchester had an active Round Table membership of thirty. This membership represented a good cross-section of everything that went on in the town. We had a banker, a butcher, a solicitor, a grocer, a timber merchant, a school teacher and a doctor, and so on. It would be hard to find any one area of Tadchester that wasn't represented by a Round Tabler.

The fortnightly meetings were pretty inebriated affairs and the guest speakers often came in for some fairly rough handling.

There was a speakers' secretary, who arranged our lecture programme. Although there were plenty of speakers available in the summer when the town was invaded by outsiders, in the winter we were thrown very much on our own resources.

The speakers' secretary arranged a series of talks where some senior member of the same profession as one of the Round Tablers was asked to come and talk about the other side of his life – his hobbies, his leisure pursuits, what he did to balance the exacting role of his work . . .

We had a fascinating talk on home movies with some home-made films illustrating it, by a senior bank manager; a talk on sailing by a senior solicitor, which wasn't too bad. It was only when he was finishing his talk that I remembered that it would be my turn to produce a senior member of my profession to speak in a fortnight's time.

I was very limited in my choice. Steve and Jack would never speak anywhere and Henry, once he had started speaking, was very difficult to stop. As for speaking myself, after the fiasco of the Cricket Club dinner I didn't think I would ever dare to raise my voice in public in Tadchester again.

There was nothing else for it. I approached Henry as my only potential speaker.

'What, lad? A talk on how doctors spend their leisure time?' (Henry always got things a bit wrong.) 'Delighted to, lad. Just leave it to me.'

With some misgiving I knew that I would have to leave it to Henry – he was a law unto himself.

Henry was late arriving for the meeting. I thought, for a time, he had forgotten, but he breezed in just after we had finished eating and in the middle of our business.

'Sorry I am late, lads,' he said. 'Just had an emergency at the hospital. All right if I start right away? I may have to shoot back there.'

Nobody ever dared to contradict Henry, not in Tadchester anyway.

Henry stood up and, without using notes or changing his expression, began his speech. I think it bears repeating:

'It is generally accepted that the doctor, whether surgeon or humble GP, is exposed to greater strains and responsibilities than his average fellow beings – the exacting toll of the operating theatre, where the saving of life is often dependent on the single skill of a particular surgeon, and general practice, where too often the only treatment required is the transfusion of the practitioner's own energy, the supply of which is not inexhaustible.

'To keep going in these exacting roles it is essential that the practising doctor has some wider interest and relaxation to distract, relax and refresh him for coming battles. In choosing his particular form of relaxation he has to be relatively selective. It is necessary that he is in a situation where he is not available to the medical demands of the general public and in a situation that will improve both his mental and physical health.

'Many splendid activities spring to mind – camping, golfing, sailing, swimming, tennis, squash and badminton – delightful sports which fill the criteria of availability and health improvement.

'For the non-sporting types there are chess, gardening, amateur dramatics, literary and art societies, television and the theatre – a whole range of available activities. It is so essential to do, or belong to, something.

'The doctor, before making his choice of activity, should scrutinise with good clinical judgement his particular distraction to assess both the obvious benefits and possible less obvious disadvantages.

'Let us look first at camping –

'What better than the wide open spaces of camping, being close to Nature, rising by the sun and going to bed when it sets, no telephone, no distractions, at peace with oneself?

'But if it rains, then you are stuck in a tent with a muddy field to walk across. If it blows, you are hanging on to the pole for dear life to keep at least some covering over your head. If it continues to rain and blow, you arrive back from your relaxation with as much vigour as a survivor from a shipwreck.

'So perhaps this should not be recommended.

'Golfing? There is no doubt about the advantages of golf. It is a splendid feeling to beat your frustrations away on the golf course. A good round will put you in fine fettle, pull you out of any sort of depression that is bothering you, and you will return to the clubhouse feeling like a king.

'But if you have a bad round everything looks black. Not only do all your other troubles heap up on you, but your golf falls apart as well. More time is spent worrying and being neurotic about golf handicaps, swings, etcetera, than all the commonplace problems we have to deal with during our work. There is no worse depression than being off your game of golf. This depression will influence every other activity you participate in.

'So perhaps this should not be recommended.

'Sailing? The wind in your face, waves swishing across the bow, scudding along in a ten-knot wind, probably the most exhilarating sport there is. You come back a giant, bronzed, full of vim and vigour.

'But, if you have a boat, you have to maintain it. You must be prepared to spend as much time working on it as in it. You have got to find a place to moor it. Masts are always snapping and sails are always tearing.

'It is expensive. It is a worry. It is a commitment. It is time-consuming. Somebody might borrow your boat or, even worse, steal it. The work problem is so involved that it interferes with any other social invitation you may have.

'So perhaps this should not be recommended.

'Swimming? Probably the best all-round sport for general health and muscular trim and shape. The refreshment of the cool waves or the leisure of a tepid swimming bath relaxes you both in body and mind.

'But, of course, you could always drown.

'So perhaps this should not be recommended.

'Tennis, badminton or squash? The main benefits of these are that you can plan to spend a specific period of time playing them. You can book a court and thrash yourself round for an hour, dispelling the accumulated toxins of the sophisticated suburban life most of us now lead. A pint of beer and a shower afterwards and you are fit to face the world.

'But, if you are a busy doctor you can't maintain your general state of body fitness. Strenuous muscular exercise concentrated in one hour of violent activity brings the muscles out on strike. The more militant ones tear themselves off their attachments, protesting in the most effective way, crippling their owner and preventing him carrying out his normal everyday tasks.

'So perhaps these should not be recommended.

'We can now examine some non-sporting activities, starting with chess –

'This is a most stimulating exercise for the mind. You can set your wits and intelligence against somebody of just about, or just less than, your equal.

'But chess is usually played with a bad posture. And usually in a smoke-filled room. It can go on for hours. Your opponent may not speak. If you keep on losing, you get into the same state of mind as the off-form golfer, and your poor chess performances begin to influence every aspect of your workaday life.

'So perhaps this should not be recommended.

'Amateur dramatics? The main benefits of amateur dramatics are that you explore those unused parts of you that you feel have been wasted. Expressing yourself in a variety of different moods can only widen your depth of understanding. You can find a new dimension here which is both enriching and stimulating. It can enhance your community standing, where people recognise both your skill as a doctor and your talents as an actor.

'But it is difficult to spare the time to go to rehearsals. Swopping duties, getting somebody to stand in for you, and usually an epidemic breaks out the week of your performance.

'Amateur dramatic societies are plagued with intrigues, splinter groups and illicit love affairs. If you are not involved in them you will be asked to help to sort them out. In time most of your worries will be concerned with:

(a) the production;
(b) whether you can get to rehearsal; and
(c) how the hell you are going to sort out the nuts you are associating with.

'So perhaps this should not be recommended.

'Gardening has many benefits. Not only are you exercising in God's fresh air, but you are doing fundamental basic things – turning the rich earth, planting seeds, seeing them flower and fruit, and benefiting from the fresh foods you have grown. It has so many branches – vegetables, flowers, greenhouse products – that you can even specialise in one particular aspect. You become closer to Nature, fitter for your exercise, and better for the fresh foods you grow.

'But, once having got your garden to a certain state, you have got to maintain it. In time you don't run your garden, your garden runs you. You can't go away on holiday because someting needs cutting or something needs picking whilst you are away. All your hopes can be dashed by too heavy a shower of rain, too much sun, or just one night of sharp frost. Having achieved a standard you will find that you require every waking moment to maintain that standard.

'So perhaps this should not be recommended.

'Art societies? Literary societies? There are many societies dedicated to the Arts which always welcome a doctor as a member. He adds status to the society by virtue of his qualifications, he has a good intellect, he can give wider advice on most subjects.

'Involvement in some pure art interest, completely separate from the mundane worries of his medical practice, can be the one thing that keeps the doctor sane, keeps his balance and equips him better to deal with his everyday patients. However hard he is pressed, he knows he can always escape into this beautiful, abstract world of culture.

'But so many societies are controlled, run and composed of rather elderly ladies. So he won't get much mental or cultural stimulation there. Because he is a doctor and known to be a responsible citizen, they will try and shove some office – either secretary or treasurer – upon him. In a short time he will find that he is running the whole affair and he cannot stop. Without his guiding hand, the society would fold up.

'Having a live doctor as secretary or treasurer does save his fellow members having to go further than the weekly society meeting for medical advice. You can bet that the doctor will spend as much time dispensing medicine as he does organising visits to art galleries, literary congresses and poetry readings.

'So perhaps this should not be recommended.

'But a doctor must relax. He must get away from it all and into tranquil surroundings. What could be more refreshing than a straightforward hysterectomy on a cool summer's afternoon, surrounded by the highly qualified theatre staff who can anticipate every instrument needed? Cut off from the outside world, doing a job that has a beginning and an end, knowing nobody will disturb you, somebody will benefit, and relaxing in familiar surroundings with familiar people.

'This is highly recommended.

'For the general practitioner there is nothing to beat a snug surgery on a cold winter's evening. The regulars coming to pay tribute at his feet, to swop yarns over bottles of urine, makes the general practitioner feel wanted and necessary. At surgery he dispenses wisdom and comfort amongst people who depend on him, working again in familiar surroundings with familiar people. Most relaxing and refreshing.

'This is highly recommended.

'So, having permutated all the possibilities, there is a way for both surgeons and general practitioners to relax – providing of course they accept that they need their patients more than perhaps their patients need them.'

There was silence for a minute after Henry stopped speaking. Then, spontaneously, the whole Table were up on their feet applauding him.

Henry beamed, soaking in the applause, then as it died

down said, 'Sorry I won't have time to answer any questions, lads. I have to shoot back to the hospital.'

He took a quick swig from the nearest beer mug, then swept out of the room.

The inimitable Henry, who always got away with everything, had got away with it again.

CHAPTER 11

Carnival Week in Tadchester rivalled Christmas as the main event of the year. The abandonment, colour and gaiety may not have been quite up to *Mardi Gras* standards, but there was enough for Tadchester. To the locals it certainly felt very Latin and more than a little wicked, especially as the population was swollen by thousands of holidaymakers and day trippers who gave the old town an added air of bustle and fiesta.

The week was the second in August, and was virtually a public holiday. Any business not connected with eating, drinking or making merry came almost to a dead stop. Traffic ground to a halt as well: the main road to the quay was blocked off to site the huge West Country Fair which provided the focus for the jollifications.

The fair was one of the good old good ones: huge, old fashioned and with something for everybody. As well as the usual dodgem cars, a big dipper, octopus and ghost train, there were dozens of sideshows – stalls offering roll-a-penny, darts, shooting, coconut shies, candy floss, fish and chips, hot dogs and hamburgers – and a boxing booth. In addition there were half a dozen large tents that set the mouths of the Tadchester locals watering. There were cries of 'Come and see the only living mermaid'! There were shows that promised exotic Eastern fantasies. One claimed to have the only Elephant Man in captivity, and there was a special one called 'Scenes from Soho', in which several rather portly ladies semi-stripped to music from an old piano.

This last show used to drive the locals wild and was responsible for many proposals of marriage: the young men seemed to think that marriage was probably the only way they could get their fantasies realised. There were others, of course, who stuck to the traditional Tadchester proposal – 'Now that you are two months gone, hadn't we better start thinking about getting married?'

The busiest man of the Tadchester Week was Eric. Apart from the fair there were the West Country rowing races on the Tad, a business exhibition in the sports ground, athletics on the cricket ground for the children, a donkey derby at Sanford-on-Sea organised by the Round Table and, most important of all, the Carnival procession.

Eric and his chief electrician, Dennis, had to provide sound and music for every event. Eric didn't speak to me for the week that the Carnival was on. He had to lay two miles of cable along the bank of the Tad, so that there could be continuous commentary on the boat races. There had to be loudspeakers, music and microphones for whoever considered themselves God's gift to broadcasting at all the other functions.

After every Carnival there were always at least half a dozen young men who were modestly lapping up the praise of 'You were such a natural on the radio, surely you are meant for the BBC.' In actual fact two Tadchester boys became internationally known as radio and TV commentators. Part of their success was due, I am sure, to their training at the Tadchester Carnival.

Pam had taken a week off to enjoy her first Carnival. She had already had one week in June when she came down to start fitting up the flat we had rented from Herbert Barlow. The second week in August would be the remainder of her holiday entitlement, and on 3rd September she was giving up work altogether to have a few days off before our marriage on the 9th.

Pam worked for *Dalton's Weekly*, an advertising magazine. For some years she was the Query Department. The proprietors of the magazine were friends of her father's. I teased her that the real reason she was marrying me was that it would enable her to come and live by the seaside and avoid the terrible journey from Leatherhead to Clapham Junction each day.

Carnival Week usually brought good weather with it. Early on the first day everybody was up and about, sniffing the prevailing excitement. Hundreds of Tadchestrians and holidaymakers patrolled the quay looking for something to take an interest in. Eric had about two hundred volunteers to assist him in his riverside cable-laying. The fair people were still putting the final touches to the stalls and sideshows and the fair lads were sniffing out the local talent, usually successfully, and inevitably leaving me with a few heartbroken cases of gonorrhoea to deal with.

Pam loved every minute of the atmosphere. There is something special about communities like Tadchester: you belonged and were part of all that went on.

I was much involved with the Carnival procession. This was well supported by Tadchester and each organisation, shop, place of work had been hard at work on their floats for weeks. I was to be on the Round Table float. We were to go in drag as Miss Tadchester 1957. I had pinched from the hospital some rolls of stockinette normally used to line plaster jackets and Bob Lording, a local tailor, had made pink body stocking suits out of them. On top of these we were to wear bikinis borrowed from wives, friends and mothers. We wore bathing hats and, apart from the odd member with a beard or moustache, looked like very presentable females.

There seemed to be hundreds of floats, stretching for miles. In fact there were seventy-two, a record entry. We were surrounded by fairies, goblins, sailors, Tom Pearce and his grey mare, people on penny-farthings, wheel-barrows, pogo sticks and every other conceivable form of transport. Some of the floats were magnificent; there was one made entirely of flowers to represent a lifeboat. There was the Carnival Queen, Barbara Jacobs, a voluptuous wench, sitting on a lorry absolutely covered in tulips.

Gwendoline Jacobs, Barbara's elder sister, had been Queen the year before. The sexiest-looking girl I had ever seen, she had been a patient of mine and a great worry to me. She would send for me to call and greet me at the door in a bikini. When she worked on the Telephone Exchange she listened in to, and interrupted, my calls. She had made a final and unsuccessful bid to get me to propose at last year's Carnival Ball. Apart from a note saying that she was now living in London working in a strip club and that there was always a bed for me there if I ever wanted one, I had not heard from her since then.

Underneath it all, Gwendoline was quite a character. There was a twinkle in her eye beneath her open sexuality. Judging from the amount of bosom Barbara was showing, she obviously shared the dominant gene that Gwendoline had inherited.

The idea was that the procession would wind its way on a five-mile route through the town, giving the locals and the holidaymakers the opportunity of throwing money on to the floats. The charity this year was Tadchester Hospital where a new X-ray machine was needed.

First we had to be judged. There were about a dozen categories of float and about six prizes for each category, Best Turned Out, Most Original, Funniest, etc., so that in fact nearly every float received some sort of prize. This in no way reduced the meticulous standard of the judging, the judges consisting of the Lady Mayoress and three or four other ladies who were heads of the various women's organisations in the town, plus the Matron of Tadchester Hospital.

These poor unfortunate women knew that they had to live on in the community after the Carnival was over. Anything slipshod in their approach, or the wrong words of praise, could make enemies and lead to feuds that would last till at least next year's Carnival. In fact, it was difficult to get people to volunteer to judge. It had been suggested at one Carnival committee meeting that the judges should be appointed like members of juries, i.e., that names should be taken at random off the electoral list and anyone not turning up for duty should be fined.

With the record entry of floats the judging took literally hours. Although it was sunny in the late afternoon when judging started, by the time it had finished a steady and heavy drizzle had begun.

One foresighted member of the Round Table had installed a barrel of beer on our float. Waiting in the rain, we were able to match the dampness falling on our outsides by continually damping our insides.

It was all too much for Harry Robinson, the dentist, full of beer and having missed his lunch by working through in order to be free for the Carnival. Surrounded by willowy, boisterous, female-looking shapes, he became a bit confused and started to proposition Jimmy Millington, the local pork butcher. Jimmy, being beardless and moustacheless, with a bathing-cap clapped firmly on his head and his wet stockinette and bikini clinging tightly to him, looked exactly the right thing to Harry. That beer *must* have been good.

At last we were off. The crowds, having had to wait as long as we had, also seemed to have been refreshing themselves with beer. Whereas the children's floats got applause and money showered on them, our bedraggled lot was their target for abuse. The rain had made most of the stockinette body suits sag and they were beginning to collect in rings around our legs. A few bras had slipped, a few bathing hats had been knocked off and we looked a bit like refugees from a brothel being run out of town by the sheriffs.

Until we came round on to the quay the abuse had been mainly verbal. However, once we were parading in front of the row of pubs that lined the quay the abuse became more material. We seemed to have every sort of object coming at us from every angle; cauliflowers, apples, oranges, bread and a few empty beer cans. Being men of some mettle and being fortified by a couple of gallons of beer apiece, we did not accept these insults lightly. Everything that hit our float was thrown back indiscriminately into the crowd. I caught a glimpse of the Lady Mayoress removing cauliflower from her chain of office. Things were beginning to get ugly and the crowd began to surge towards our float with the obvious intention of taking it apart.

Police Sergeant Jenkins moved forward to make a barrier between the two lots of potential combatants. At this moment Bob Lording hit him full in the face with an ill-directed beer can and Sergeant Jenkins went down with blood pouring from his forehead. Seeing his condition, I leapt off the float to attend to him. I could see the cut was only superficial and that the fall had been aggravated by the sergeant's stepping on some wet cabbage. He was fully compos mentis, shouting, 'I saw who did that! I'll book you for that!'

The Round Table, sensing danger, started to shuffle about, changing their position on the float. There was no chance of anyone recognising anyone.

The crowd was silent and stunned at first. Then what started as a trickle of laughter steadily increased into a roar.

'Thank God,' I thought as I pressed my thumb on the bleeding point of the sergeant's face. 'Something has distracted them.'

I turned to see what they were laughing at. Couldn't be the float – that had disappeared into the distance. It was me! In jumping from the float, my strapless bra had slipped to my waist and the bottom half of my bikini had followed the path of the soggy wet stockinette and was situated somewhere around my knees. It was in this situation that I was bending over the police sergeant, pressing my thumb on his forehead.

The sergeant brushed my hand away, got up and, adjusting his helmet above his blood-stained face, went off growling, 'Bloody lot of nancy boys! Someone is going to pay for this . . .'

I was rescued by Pam and Gladys who, with tears of laughter running down their faces, pushed their way through the crowd bearing a raincoat and said, 'Come on, put this on and let's get you out of here.'

Just after we left, the drizzle turned into a downpour and the whole procession was abandoned in chaos.

Pam loved Carnival Week; Tadchester was alive and there was something going on all the time. We sat on the bank of the River Tad to watch the West Country rowing championship. Tadchester, being Tadchester, had two rowing clubs: the Reds and the Blues. It was much more important to beat the local opposition than it was to triumph over other clubs like Brixham and Torquay. The Reds won the championship with the Blues coming a poor third.

After the regatta we went for a meal with Janice and

Kevin Bird. Kevin was the farm manager for the de Wyrebocks and always kept open house for me. Janice looked a bit down during dinner and eventually, after a lot of probing, admitted that she had a stomach pain. 'Come on, Janice,' I said, 'let's get you upstairs and have a look at you.'

Janice was plump, in fact quite plump. She kept some of her contours down with various belts and supports. Kevin, watching her get dressed one morning, saw her put on some pants followed by a roll-on, followed by stockings and suspender belt, followed by some long johns.

'If you should by chance get raped today,' said Kevin, 'whoever does it deserves a medal.'

It took a while for Janice to disrobe, but eventually she lay on the bed presenting a vast expanse of white abdomen for me to have a go at. I wasn't quite sure where to begin.

'If your hands are cold,' said Janice, 'I'll scream.'

I turned away and washed my hands under the hot tap. When I came back to have a look at Janice's abdomen, things had changed. The broad white expanse now had a series of regular black marks running across it from the top right corner to the bottom left. I couldn't make it out. For some reason, Janice lay there giggling. When I looked more closely at the marks, they appeared to be some sort of muddy rubber stamp. There were several points on each mark, and by rubbing one of them I found I could remove the muddy-coloured substance to leave faint scratch marks underneath.

Before I washed my hands her abdomen had been spotless. I wondered if this could be instant shingles or some other rare condition.

'Janice,' I asked, 'how on earth did you get these marks?'

She burst out laughing.

'Oh Bob,' she said, 'while you were washing your hands, the cat came through the window, jumped on the bed, walked straight across my stomach then shot out through the door.'

I laughed with her, wondering why the cat should have walked across her stomach with its claws out; perhaps it was my hand-washing in the corner that had put it on edge.

I could find nothing amiss with Janice's stomach and she was fit enough to go with us to the fair in the evening. We were joined by Frank Squires, his wife Primrose, and Eric and Zara, and set off in high spirits to explore the attractions.

Kevin said, 'Why not pop in to the fortune teller, Janice, and have your stomach read? She might welcome a change from palms.'

We sampled most of what was going on – the dodgem cars, the big dipper, the octopus and a whole variety of things that went up and down and round and round.

'Now for the tents,' said Frank.

We had a good laugh at the Soho Strippers. The tent seemed full of youths who had attended me regularly for their acne. In the boxing booth we were greeted by Jack Dawson, the ex-hangman.

'Do you fancy a few rounds with me, doctor?' said Jack.

Jack, true to tradition, had spent the first half of Carnival Week knocking out all the booth professionals and was now employed to help them see the week through. He had few challengers and was a bit too big and strong for most of them. At one time he had been a contender for the professional heavyweight championship.

The Elephant Man was a disappointment. He had some sort of trunk, admittedly; a roll of flesh coming down from the middle of his forehead in a loop – but it was certainly not elephantine.

My medical curiosity was aroused, however. How did he get a loop of flesh like that? I decided to ask, and when the tent was quiet, walked over to him.

He put out his hand. 'Nice to see you, Dr Clifford,' he said. 'I hope you haven't forgotten me. I was under your care at St Chad's. I can never thank you for what you did for me. I've been able to make a steady living ever since.'

Suddenly I remembered. When I was the plastic surgery house surgeon at St Chad's we had a patient who had lost his nose through some congenital disease. The plastic surgeon had attempted to rebuild one for him. It was a complicated process. First the patient's upper arm had to be attached to his forehead. When the living pedicle of flesh had been established between arm and forehead, the part attached to the arm was severed and the severed end was then sewn into the area where the plastic re-moulding was to take place.

Charley Harrow, the Elephant Man, had had some trouble with the lower end of his pedicle graft. It should have taken root in the nasal area, but for some reason it didn't. Charley was due to have it re-stitched when he disappeared from the ward. How in his condition he managed to get out, we never knew. He certainly had no clothes in the ward and, to say the least, he was certainly not inconspicuous.

'When are you going back to have it all finished up?' I said to Charley.

'Only if the money dries up,' he replied. 'It's a good income. They aren't very keen on me when I go into pubs, but,' he said with a twinkle, 'it doesn't put the ladies off – they think I've got spares.'

The last tent of all contained the only living mermaid in captivity. Sitting on a rock in a tank was a half-naked girl with long blonde hair hanging down to her waist from where a plastic tail took over.

What did seem incongruous was that the mermaid was wearing sunglasses. And there was something familiar about her. Those bosoms – surely I had seen them some-where before, but they didn't fit in with the long blonde hair. I stared and stared trying to make up my mind. Pam was always saying that I thought I recognised everybody. Anyway, I gave it up and after a nightcap in The Goat, we called it a day.

Next day, in the surgery, on my desk was a scented envelope and a letter in large childish handwriting. It read, 'Dear Dr Bob, Thank you for not giving me away. I had to dye my hair blonde when I knew we were coming to Tadchester. They tell me you are getting married soon. What a pity. Could you see me tomorrow at the fairground? My caravan is the blue one to the right of the big dipper. Please come. I'm in terrible trouble and I need your help.'

There were three large kisses at the bottom of the letter and it was signed *Gwendoline Jacobs* . . .

CHAPTER 12

The next day, after surgery, I drove my car to the fairground. The Carnival was over and the fair had lost all the bustle and gaiety of the previous week. Stalls and roundabouts were being dismantled and council workmen were beginning to cart away the week's accumulation of rubbish and refuse.

There were dozens of traction engines and lorries parked all over the place with no sense of order and I could not find Gwendoline's caravan. Eventually I stopped one of the fairground hands and asked if he could point out Miss Jacobs's caravan. He didn't seem to know her name.

'She is the lady in the tank,' I said, trying to be helpful.

'You mean our f . . . . . . mermaid,' he replied with a leer. 'She's parked out just beyond the fruit machine arcade, next to the big dipper.' He smiled knowingly. 'You're chancing your arm a bit aren't you, guv?'

Secretly I had been rather looking forward to seeing Gwendoline. She had always been quite a character, overtly sexual, but retaining a twinkle in her eye as if she were only really teasing and knew the rules as well as anyone else.

The insinuations of the fairground hand worried me. I began to smell trouble . . .

Gwendoline's caravan was in a poor state of repair, with the paintwork cracked and fading. The blue was no longer a true blue but had a sort of washed-out look about it.

Gwendoline opened the door to my knock. She said, 'Thank God you've come, doctor. Do come in.'

The poorly lit caravan was just as tawdry inside. There was an unmade bed at one end and a few broken-down chairs at the other. The small sink was piled with unwashed dishes. Gwendoline was wearing an old dressing-gown loosely held at the waist by a cord, loose enough for me to see that she wore nothing at all underneath. She wore sunglasses, as she had in the tank. Her long, dyed blonde hair tumbled down, unbrushed, over her shoulders and looked unkempt and out of condition. I felt very ill at ease.

'What can I do for you, Gwendoline?' I asked.

She shrugged her shoulders, then muttered, 'We'll have some coffee first.'

She turned to the sink, cleared away some of the pots and pumped some water into a tin kettle which she put on the gas stove. I tried to make light conversation, enquiring after her family and asking what had happened to her since she left Tadchester. She replied in monosyllabic grunts. My questions struck no sparks, brought forth none of the bubbling answers I expected. She stood with her back to me, watching the gas ring, her cigarette stuck to her lower lip as if it had been attached by adhesive. This was not the vivacious Gwendoline of twelve months ago.

The grunts gave way to no answers at all, and I abandoned my attempts at conversation. The whistle of the boiling kettle brought Gwendoline out of her reverie. She turned off the gas, wiped clean two mugs from the pile in the sink, put a teaspoon of instant coffee in each, poured in water from the kettle, added some milk from a bottle she picked out of the clutter, then came towards me with the steaming mugs.

She sat down facing me. Her loosely tied dressing-gown was half open and her nakedness looked somehow vulgar in the half light. We sipped our coffee without speaking. Every instinct in me was shouting 'Get up and get out of here!' Foolishly, I did not.

I broke the silence with my original question. 'What can I do for you, Gwendoline?'

Gwendoline didn't respond for a moment or two, except to put her coffee mug down on the dirty carpeting of the van. Then she got up, walked to the door and pressed a switch. The caravan was flooded with a harsh neon light from a tube in the centre of the ceiling. Gwendoline took off her glasses and slid her dressing-gown from her shoulders. It fell around her ankles.

I had my first proper look at her. She had aged twenty years since I had last seen her. She was unwashed, there were dirt rings on her legs and thighs. There were dark shadows under both eyes and her once-perfect breasts drooped above a distended pot-like stomach. This sagging body was framed by her dyed hair, hanging crinkly and unkempt. There were strange mottled marks on both forearms. She looked like some strange Macbethian hag.

Gwendoline had been queen of the castle in Tadchester, but London had obviously been too much even for her quite considerable resilience. She was a broken shell of the girl of last year. The Smoke had taken its toll.

The girl was obviously no longer in balance with herself. She had 'flipped'. And I had a big problem on my hands.

I repeated my question brusquely and professionally. 'What can I do for you, Gwendoline?'

She half simpered. 'I want to do a trade with you, Doctor Bob.' She smiled, edging towards me.

'What do you mean, a trade?'

'Well, Doctor Bob,' she said, 'you always had an eye for the girls, and presumably you've still got it. I need a fix. There's nothing loose in this bloody town. You are my only hope – you can prescribe anything you want. For God's sake – you can do whatever you like with me – and I mean whatever – but in return I want some heroin . . .'

The marks on her forearm now made sense – Gwendoline was taking heroin intravenously. Drug addicts were relatively rare at this time; if they *were* addicted, then it was to something pretty tough. Soft drugs were not abused then, as they were to become some years later.

'This is silly,' I said. 'You need some help. Let me fix up for someone to see you.'

I got up, heading for the door. Gwendoline, naked, stood in my way.

'Oh no you don't!' she snapped, and by now any pretence of pleasantry had gone. She snarled at me. 'A lot of people have seen you come into this caravan. I can ruin you in this town if I want to.'

'Don't be silly, Gwendoline,' I repeated. 'Let me help you. I have a friend who specialises in drug addiction. I can make an appointment for you to see him. You'll get nowhere by carrying on like this.'

I was now pushing against her, trying to get to the door. She clung to my arm and started to scream. I fought my way through, wrenched open the door, disengaged her hand and stumbled down the steps. She stood at the door, completely naked, screaming, 'Rapist bastard! I'll fix you – you see if I don't!'

Most of the fairground hands had stopped work on their dismantling and stood watching me as I made my way with as much dignity as I could towards my car. Nobody said a word, but I felt as if a thousand eyes were on me. Worse, I could still hear Gwendoline's piercing screams as I got into the car and drove away.

Now it was Question Time. How had I got into this situation? I had been foolish in that I had not registered the visit to Gwendoline in the surgery book, and the surgery didn't know where I was. I had to admit to myself I had secretly been rather looking forward to seeing Gwendoline. Vanity, I suppose.

I had read about other doctors in situations like this, but I had never envisaged that anything possibly like it could happen to me. For the first time I realised how vulnerable doctors were when they visited lady patients in their own homes.

I wondered if Gwendoline really would try to make trouble for me. Half the fairground staff had seen me leaving the caravan, with Gwendoline standing naked and screaming at the door. The fairground hand I'd asked directions from had half warned me. What a fool I'd been . . .

I called in at Eric's shop on the way to the surgery.

'Christ, what a mess!' he said. (Thanks a bunch, I thought. Nothing like a few comforting words from an old friend in times of trouble.)

'It's her word against yours,' Eric went on. 'But that's not the only point – if a hint of it gets into the press, as a doctor you're crucified whether you've done anything or not. I've had some of the same sort of trouble when I've been called to television breakdowns. I've found some-times that it's the lady of the house, not the set, that needs rewiring. But I'm not a doctor, thank God, and I have my own language for dealing with these situations.'

I went back to the surgery in despair. I just didn't know what to do.

Gladys remarked, 'You do look down in the dumps today, Doctor Bob.' I raised as much of a smile as I could muster and went to my room where I sat thinking.

Whom could I talk to about this? It was laughable in one way but deadly serious in another. As Eric said – get a hint of this in the papers and, innocent as I was, they'd have me. I imagined the headlines:

THE DOCTOR AND THE MERMAID
'HE RAPED ME,' SAYS FAIRGROUND BLONDE

Steve, with whom I would normally talk over problems like this, was away on holiday. I was sure it would upset Pam, who was up to her eyes in wedding preparations. She would sympathise and stand by me, but practically she would not be able to advise. The situation would add yet one more worry to her list.

Henry Johnson would have laughed his head off. 'Just forget it,' he would say. 'She's a nut. Nothing's going to happen.' Henry had several times been put in the situation that I was in. He had just laughed it off, and that was that. But everything was like that with Henry.

I could not rid myself of this foreboding of trouble. Jean Hart, Jack's wife, was seriously ill in hospital, so I couldn't bother him. I was thrown back on my own resources and was frightened to discover how inadequate they were. I racked my brains. What could I do? Then I thought of Marion Cook.

Marion Cook was Tadchester's most prominent citizen. She was the town's first lady mayor, a JP, chairman of the governors of the grammar school, a member of a BBC advisory committee, and a *cordon bleu* cook. But above all else, this talented and tirelessly active woman always seemed to have time for people with worries and problems.

Marion was about the only person who would make herself cheerfully available for tiresome, tedious jobs like signing passports. She had been a great help to many of my patients in all sorts of emotional, economic and family upsets. I rang her and tentatively explained my problem. My story sounded very stupid as I told it over the phone, but Marion was instantly both compassionate and practical.

'Oh you poor thing,' she said. 'As if you doctors don't have enough to cope with. You must take this seriously, Bob: unbalanced people do unbalanced things. Now leave it to me. Come round for a cup of coffee at about eight this evening. I'll see what I can do.'

The fact that my problem was now shared, and shared with someone of Marion's stature, was a tremendous relief. I got through my day's work with half my mind still on the problem of Gwendoline, and duly reported to Marion at eight o'clock. She kissed me on the cheek.

'Come in and stop worrying,' she said. 'I have someone in the lounge I want you to discuss your problem with.'

Sitting in the lounge was the uniformed Inspector Harold, the head of the Tadchester Constabulary. Marion had been to work. It was difficult to believe that what had started off as a problem-free day was developing into a situation involving the town's mayor and head of police. Marion introduced us.

'Bob,' she said, 'perhaps you would tell your story to Inspector Harold. I have not discussed anything with him: I have just asked him round as a friend to give help and advice to another friend.'

Inspector Harold did not look in the least pleased to be there. Wearing his uniform was probably part of his protest. It would be difficult, nigh impossible, to refuse an invitation from the forceful Marion. She was so involved with everything that virtually everybody was dependent on her. Her word was, in fact, almost law. No head of law enforcement could possibly like that.

I told my story to Inspector Harold, feeling completely foolish. He sat perfectly still, his face expressionless. He made no comment until I had finished. With no attempt to encourage or reassure me in any way, he then said, 'A part of your story I already know. Strictly off the record' (he coughed and looked at Marion, embarrassed), 'Miss Jacobs called at the police station this morning to lay a complaint of physical assault and attempted rape against you. We know Miss Jacobs and we know you. The complaint was noted, but for our part we do not intend to take any further action.'

His face gave away nothing, but I remembered Eric's words in the morning: 'Once this gets about, however innocent you are, as a doctor you're crucified . . .'

I saw, or thought I saw, a sort of 'There's no smoke without fire' look behind the Inspector's lack of expression.

'What do you suggest I do?' I asked.

'There's nothing the police can do,' he snapped back. 'If you want to take out a civil summons against her, that is entirely your affair. It is not without its own complications and it's nothing to do with the police.'

He got up, ready to go. He was obviously dying for his supper and thought that all this was a terrible waste of time.

'You mean you can't help?' said Marion, in a steely voice which hinted that whatever functions she was going to patronise during her term of office, the Police Ball would not be one of them.

'I'm very sorry, Madam Mayor,' said the Inspector. 'There's nothing I can do. I have already exceeded my responsibilities by informing you of the complaint laid. If you'll excuse me, I will be on my way now.'

'He lacks the courage of his predecessor,' said Marion after she had seen him out. 'If old Inspector Watts had been here he would have sorted it all out in a jiff.'

I sat back in my chair, dazed. Things now seemed worse, not better – I had been reported to the police for attempted rape. Marion saw my concern.

'Do stop worrying, Bob,' she said. 'You have done

nothing. I'll have to sort this out on my own. Now you sit down in front of the television and relax. I'm going out – I'm going to lay this ghost tonight.'

She put on her hat and coat, and slipped out of the door. A few minutes later I heard her car drive away.

I sat in front of the television, not watching, with the sound turned down so that I would catch the noise of her returning car. I felt like a helpless child, with Mother going out to sort out my troubles.

It was an an hour before Marion returned. She was steely faced and tense – but obviously something had been done.

'Well, Bob,' she said, 'you can forget all about your little problem. Gwendoline will be off in the morning, the matter's closed. So forget it and stop worrying about it – and I mean stop *worrying* about it.'

'What happened?' I asked.

'What happened,' said Marion, 'is my secret. Let's say that this town appointed me as its mayor to ensure that there is justice and order in the community. Tonight I have been out in pursuance of that trust. Apart from that, the matter is closed.'

The traumas of that night, when I benefited so much from Marion's good offices, were the beginning of a long and valued friendship with her. The next morning, as she had predicted, the fair had gone, taking Gwendoline with it. It was a tremendous relief to me. I called on Marion with a bunch of flowers, feeling that this was the least I could do. I again tried to broach the subject of what had happened the night before. Marion looked stern.

'Bob,' she said, 'the matter is really closed.' Then she relaxed and said, 'One day, when you write your book, you will be able to put all this down.'

And now, as I write my book, I can pay tribute to Marion Cook, first Lady Mayor of Tadchester . . . and Woman Extraordinary.

CHAPTER 13

Two weeks after the Carnival I was called to see Janice
Bird. Of all my friends she seemed to be the unluckiest
with her health. She had been very ill the previous year
when she was one of several people who were infected by
eating diseased pork. From what Kevin had said on the
phone, she was complaining of the same sort of symptoms.

The patients who had been infected by the pork all
confessed to eating it uncooked, mainly by eating a pinch
of raw sausage meat when spicing it. Surely Janice had
learnt her lesson?

Things weren't too bad when I saw her. She was feverish
and had a headache. As soon as I came through the door
she said, 'Sorry to call you in, Bob. And before you ask –

I definitely haven't eaten any raw sausage meat.'

When I examined her I found that her temperature was raised and that she had several very large glands in her right groin. There were a few small glands in the left groin, and a few under each arm and in her neck. Apart from the glands in the groin her other glands didn't seem to be affected.

'I think you have glandular fever,' I said to Janice. 'I'll do a blood test to confirm it, not that it will make any difference; the condition will get better on its own. I can't say how long you are going to feel unwell, but it's likely to be at least a week and possibly several.'

I took some blood and called again in a couple of days. To my surprise Janice seemed completely recovered. Also her blood tests had come back negative to glandular fever.

My provisional diagnosis was wrong, but, as I said to Janice, I had to prove what she didn't have as a first step to discovering what in fact she did have.

The glands in her right groin were as big as ever. I examined the leg to see if there were any infected cuts that could be causing them, but it was quite clear and there was no obvious reason why she should have these glands.

'OK, Janice,' I said, 'you can get up and about, but I want to see you each week until these glands have gone down or disappeared.'

I subsequently saw Janice every week for four weeks. She was perfectly well but her glands still remained and I thought a couple of them were even a little bigger. I began to wonder if these were signs of something more sinister, so I made an appointment for her to see my physician friend John Bowler at the Winchcombe Hospital.

He rang me after he had seen Janice. 'I don't know what they are,' he said. 'I'll have to get one of my surgical colleagues to remove one and send it to Pathology.' Janice felt we were making an awful fuss, but we arranged that she should go in as a day case and have a gland removed.

A week later John rang again. 'It seems pretty good news for Janice,' he said. 'The gland is not quite typical; we think it's toxoplasmosis. This is a self-limiting disease and it will do her no harm. If the blood tests confirm it, then she can forget all about it.'

The blood tests unfortunately did not confirm this diagnosis and the pathologist at Winchcombe felt it was possible that she had a cancer of the lymph glands. He had found it difficult to establish what the gland was, so was sending slides off to St Bartholomew's Hospital in London for a further opinion. I made light of this to Janice, and anyway she felt so well that my continued fussing was all a bit of a nuisance.

The fact that Janice had a lump made all my other friends search round to see if they could find some of their own. On the same day I had both Lee – Joe Church's wife – and Frank Squires in to see me.

Lee had a painless lump in her right thigh. I'd never seen anything like it before. An X-ray of her leg was clear, so there was no obvious bone involvement, but she still had her lump. I thought it was most likely a muscular tear or a thrombosed vein, but I couldn't take a chance so I made an appointment for her to see the faithful John Bowler at Winchcombe.

Frank had a hard lump on the left side of his neck. I tried to hide my concern as I examined it. The lump was hard and fixed – it could be a sign of all sorts of nasty things. There was nothing for me to do but to bother John Bowler once again. I hoped he wasn't going to get fed up seeing all my lumpy friends.

John was on the phone to me after he had seen Lee and Frank.

'Bob,' he said, 'both of these could be nasty. I'll have to fix up for them to come in next week for biopsies. What's happening to you all in Tadchester – are you just trying to worry me to death?'

The day Lee and Frank were admitted to Winchcombe Hospital was my half day, so I went over to Winchcombe to keep an eye on them. The surgeon who was going to do the biopsies invited me to attend the operations and I went round with him for his last look at both Lee and Frank before he operated. He examined Lee's leg carefully. 'Just a torn muscle I think, my dear,' he said, 'we can put that right.'

'Frank is better off than I am,' said Lee. 'I can lose a leg – at least they won't chop his head off.'

The surgeon smiled. When we got outside I said, 'Thank goodness you think it's only a torn muscle.'

'It isn't all I think,' he replied brusquely. 'I think it's most likely that this is a very malignant kind of muscle cancer. We may, in fact, have to take her leg off.'

'You can't!' I said, horrified.

I hadn't even thought of this as possible and neither had Lee, in spite of her parting joke.

'If the biopsy shows it to be as bad as you think it is, then *she* must decide whether her leg comes off or not,' I said. 'The outlook is poor anyway. She mustn't be allowed to go to theatre thinking that she is having a muscle repaired and wake up to find she has a leg missing.'

'She won't do that,' said the surgeon. 'If it's necessary to remove her leg, we'll bring her round and discuss it with her before we proceed. Meanwhile I have an orthopaedic surgeon standing by.'

When Lee's leg was opened, the surgeon cut down and exposed a mucus-filled cyst. He removed the cyst, then snapped at the theatre sister: 'Send this for a frozen section and ask the orthopaedic surgeon to come up to the theatre.'

I protested again. 'You can't!'

The surgeon cut me short.

'A consent for operation has been signed,' he said. 'The only chance for this girl, if the cyst is malignant, is to remove her leg. This is my responsibility and my decision –

but of course we will do nothing radical until we have consulted her.'

We left Lee in the theatre with the anaesthetist, came out into the doctors' room and had a cup of tea and a smoke while we waited for the result of the frozen section. The wait seemed endless. I was thinking of how I would have to go and tell Joe that Lee had lost a leg. It was all too terrible to consider. At last came a call from the Path. Lab. No obvious malignancy on frozen section: a full opinion would be available in about a week.

'Thank God,' I thought. 'Whatever happens from now on, she'll at least have a say in whether she loses her leg or not.'

Frank's operation was without any of the drama of Lee's. The lump was bigger than first thought and the surgeon, after fiddling for about an hour, produced a round white object like a small potato from deep down in Frank's neck.

'I've never seen one of these before,' he said. 'Looks like a neuroma. It's attached to a nerve, anyway. It all looks quite harmless, but we'll have to see what the Path. Lab. thinks about it. Anyway, there's no reason why your friend shouldn't go home tomorrow, and we will let you know the final results in about a week.'

I had a restless week. Frank had lost his voice, either because of the anaesthetic or because they had to cut a nerve to get the lump out. It could have been the nerve that supplied the vocal cords, though the surgeon didn't think so at the time. They checked Frank's cords for movement after the operation and they all seemed quite happy about the way they moved.

Frank's wife, Primrose, said that it was the quietest the house had been for years. She was in no hurry for him to get his voice back.

I'd heard nothing from the Path. Lab. after seven days,

so I started to ring in each day, trying not to sound too concerned. Frank's potato, which I hadn't been very concerned about, now began to worry me. Each time I spoke to the technician at the Path. Lab. he would say, 'I'm sorry sir, we are still making further sections of the specimen; we have not made a decision yet,' There was still no news of Lee's cyst, and nothing had come from Bartholomew's Hospital about Janice's gland.

Joe, Kevin and Primrose would ring me each day on some pretext, then casually in conversation, as if it were of no consequence at all, each would say 'Is there any news yet?' They were obviously worried to death and there was little I could say to reassure them.

I made my usual daily routine call to the Path. Lab. This time the phone was answered by the pathologist and not the technician. I asked, holding my breath, if there was any news of Lee's and Frank's specimens.

'Yes,' said the pathologist, 'we have had difficulty in identifying Mr Squires' tumour; we've decided to call it a swanoma.'

'Is it malignant?' I asked.

'Oh no,' he replied. 'There's never been any suggestion that it could have been malignant. It's an unusual lump and difficult to put a name to.'

I could have thumped him for my ten days of needless worry.

'And Mrs Church?' I asked.

'Oh yes,' he said, 'another interesting case. A simple mucus-filled myxoma. If she's had one, she may have others here and there, but there's nothing to do about them – they are quite harmless.'

I could have wept with relief. Two down and one to go. If only I could get Janice's results through, life could resume some sort of normal pattern. It is so difficult treating friends, you tend to overtreat and it is difficult not to show your anxiety.

At last John Bowler came on the phone with Janice's

results. I held my breath. John chuckled. 'Bob, does Mrs Bird by any chance have a cat?'

'Yes, definitely,' I said, remembering the muddy scratch marks across her stomach.

'Well,' he said, 'she must take care in future. These glands show that what she is suffering from is cat-scratch fever. Tell her cat to keep its claws in in future.'

I sat down, exhausted. Three of my closest friends whom I was putting at death's door a fortnight ago were all completely clear.

We decided that Pam would give an after-lump dinner-party at our new flat. It wasn't completely furnished yet but there were enough chairs to go round. Pam produced a superb roast, the first meal she had cooked in Tadchester. Frank's voice was almost back to normal: it wouldn't be long before he was shouting orders to us, his slaves on the seine fishing-nets. Lee, who had still a slight limp, said, 'Bob, if my lump was a myxoma and they say I could have more, would that mean I've got myxomatosis?'

Kevin said, 'Well, you always did have rabbit teeth.'

It would be difficult to envisage a fictitious situation where three close friends should all produce some rare medical disease at the same time. I knew of cat-scratch fever but had never seen or even heard about swanomas and myxomas. I rang John Bowler.

'John,' I said, 'do you think I ought to go on a post-graduate course? I've never heard of conditions like swanomas and myxomas.'

'Don't worry,' said John, 'I've never come across them before either, but no more lumps for a bit, please – they can't all have happy endings.'

When I left medical school they had not warned me of the dangers from animals in general practice. Since coming to Tadchester, I had been attacked by pretty well every sort of domestic animal except the proverbial bull.

Mrs Chilcott was one of my nuisance patients. She was

always sending for me with some terrifying tale of illness. When I got to her house I would find her fully dressed and powdered, sporting three strings of pearls, and I would then have to listen to a monologue of how important her late husband had been, and all the important people she knew and the famous places she had been to.

She often forgot why she had sent for me. I recognised that hers was a cry for help; she was lonely and bored and I did not begrudge too much the time that I spent with her. It was as important as giving out pills or medicine. What I *did* begrudge was the guerrilla warfare conducted by her small Pekingese, Charles.

I am rather apprehensive about dogs. The dogs sense my feelings and this brings out all their nasty aggressive habits. Small dogs I didn't mind too much; I could usually block their attacks with my medical case.

Charles was different. I was completely on edge whenever I went into the house. He would launch his attack from behind settees, doors, chairs, anything that gave him some sort of cover. I never let my case out of my hand at Mrs Chilcott's. I knew that I would have to use it as a shield at any moment. I developed a technique of moving the case smartly towards Charles as he launched his attack, landing him a few fairly heavy bumps on the nose.

'Isn't he a marvellous house dog?' gushed Mrs Chilcott every time I fended off an attack. I longed to put my boot into this little monster, small as he was.

Mrs Chilcott sent for me one day. She was in bed with flu. She would leave the back door on the latch and see that Charles was safely restrained. 'Just let yourself in, doctor, I'll be in the first bedroom on the right.'

I made her my first call, purely to get it over with. Having let myself in, with case at the ready I stealthily walked to the first bedroom on the right, as Mrs Chilcott had directed. There was no sign of Charles anywhere.

Mrs Chilcott was sitting up in bed, powdered and

perfumed, still wearing her three rows of pearls on top of her nightdress. There was some preliminary talk about her condition, then I put my case down, got out my stethoscope and bent to listen to her chest. No sooner had my stethoscope touched her than out from under the eiderdown came hurtling the spitting, snarling Charles, determined to do me some actual bodily harm. He came out like a rocket, straight for my left hand. Fortunately, although I had put my case down I had unconsciously geared my reflexes and snatched my hand away just in time to miss his teeth.

Charles was unable to check his flight and sailed on, sinking his teeth into Mrs Chilcott's right breast. She shrieked – and the genteel manners and conversation that she had built up over the years were lost in a few minutes of the most blistering language that it has ever been my lot to hear. She gave precious Charles the belt round the rear end that I had been longing to give him, and shot him off the bed. This was a turning-point in my visits to Mrs Chilcott; it became quite a pleasure to go and see her. Charles, now broken-spirited, would greet me effusively whenever I called, and strenuously attempt to lick the parts that before he used to try and bite.

The Sunset Nursing Home, in Craven Hill Road, was quite different. This was a private house that offered accommodation to eight elderly ladies. They had a room each and were well cared for. The house rules, to qualify for admission, were that the patient must be ambulant, must be able to dress herself and mustn't be incontinent. Whenever I managed to get a patient admitted they seemed to behave well for a month, then go into a decline, take to their beds and become incontinent. It was to the great credit of the proprietors that they took all this in their stride and looked after their old ladies with affection and care.

I did not know how they were staffed dog-wise until one

day, visiting a patient there, I had to go in and see Mr and Mrs Reynolds who ran the Home. 'Come in,' they called, when I knocked on the door of their flatlet. I opened the door to see two gigantic Great Danes leaping off the settee to greet me and just had time to shut the door again before they reached it.

I was chided by the Reynolds. 'Oh, doctor, they wouldn't hurt a fly – they were only saying hello.' I had heard all this many times before when patients had shouted, 'Just ignore the dog, doctor, and come up.' It had cost me three pairs of trousers. I knew that the dogs by now were aware that I was scared of them, and however gentle they might be with anyone else, would vent any aggressiveness on me.

From then on, before each visit to the Home, I would ring up and warn Mr and Mrs Reynolds to shut the dogs away before I called. One day, I forgot to give my warning call, marched into the room of the patient I'd called to see, and started to examine her.

For some reasons, probably practical ones, the beds in Sunset House were very close to the ground. To examine my lady patient I had to kneel at the side of her bed. With my stethoscope in my ears I was oblivious to sounds outside. The first intimation that the dogs were not locked up was feeling hot breath on the back of my head and a large wet tongue starting to lick the back of my neck.

I dared not make a sudden move. These dogs were as big as horses. They could easily have picked me up by the scruff of my neck and shaken me. I conducted the most meticulous and thorough examination of a chest that I have ever carried out. For thirty-five minutes I listened carefully and intently to my old lady. All my movements were slow and deliberate so as not to arouse the monster that was poised literally a hair's breadth behind me. After what seemed an eternity, I heard the dog pad away. I got up stiffly, and my lady patient beamed.

'You are a marvellous doctor,' she said. 'Nobody has taken time and trouble like this with me before.'

In a fit of generosity one day I offered to do a visit for Jack Hart who was a bit pressed. I realised it was a mistake when I pulled up at a large gate which had written on it 'Beware of the Bull Mastiff'. There was no turning back. I hooted my horn just in case there was anyone about, but the gates were separated from the house by a two-hundred-yard drive and nobody came.

I slipped out of the car, pushed the gate open, then jumped back into the car. I left the gate open, hoping selfishly that if the bull mastiff was loose in the grounds it would take the opportunity of running out into the road. I drove up as close as I could to the front door of the house and looked round. No sign of a dog anywhere. I jumped out of the car into a corner of the porch, back to the wall and my case in front of me, and rang the doorbell. In the distance I could hear a muffled roar, which could have come from nothing smaller than a lion. I was let into the house, saw my patient who had been hurt in a hunting accident, then began to make my way down the stairs. As I reached the bottom, I heard a terrifying growling sound. There, framed in a doorway, was a twelve-year-old girl doing her best to restrain the biggest dog I had ever seen in my life. It could have eaten the two Great Danes for breakfast.

The girl was gasping for breath in her effort to restrain the great beast. She panted 'I would go as quickly as you can, doctor. Dinky doesn't like strangers and I don't think I can hold him much longer.'

I threw all dignity to the winds and was out of the front door and into my car in a flash. I determined never to volunteer for visits in unreconnoitred territory again.

It was not only dogs that tried to attack me. I was chased

by geese, butted by a goat, kicked by a donkey and had my finger bitten by a pet macaw. Cats, which I don't like, never bothered me; that is, they never actually attacked me. But because they sensed I didn't like them, cats always made a tremendous fuss, climbing all over me, depositing hairs all over my jacket, to the coos of their owners who would say, 'Oh, she's taken a liking to you, doctor. They can always tell a cat lover when they see one.'

I knew that whatever profession outside medicine I might have attempted, the one I would never have been able to contemplate was that of a vet.

The dangers from animals were not limited to their aggressiveness. Although I never caught anything from a pet myself, my patients seemed to be doing it all the time. I had one family of four, all down with pneumonia at the same time. I couldn't understand it; I had never heard of epidemic pneumonia. It was only on my second visit to the house that I realised what was happening.

The mother of the house greeted me with tears streaming down her face.

'Oh, doctor,' she said, 'all our parrots are dying. Do you think they have caught something from us?'

I went round the back of the house to an aviary in a shed. It was a pathetic sight. There were about two dozen dead and dying parrots on the floor. They were the root of the problem. It was the parrots that had infected the family, passing on a disease called psittacosis.

Hamsters and rabbits passed on all sorts of cystic worm infections and we even traced one source of dysentery to a tortoise. One of Henry Johnson's patients with a pet monkey nearly died of monkey-bite fever and one of Steve Maxwell's patients actually caught foot-and-mouth disease when there was an outbreak amongst the local cattle.

I said to Steve one day that I was coming to the conclusion that all pets were lethal and as far as I could see were harbingers of infection and disease.

Steve smiled. 'Well, Bob,' he said, 'I've never had much trouble with goldfish, but don't get too over-confident with them – they might easily give you a nasty suck.'

FIRST THE GOOD NEWS,
YOU HAVEN'T GOT PILES.

SURGERY

CHAPTER 14

Joe Church had become progressively restless. He was fed
up with teaching and fed up with the confines of a small
town like Tadchester – or, as he called it, Main Street.

He realised that he could never progress beyond being
games master in a grammar school and that the job in
Tadchester was as pleasant as he could expect anywhere
else. He felt that his life had come to a stop. Apart from
his fishing, rugby playing and other outside activities, life
was just a tedious routine.

We used to debate this endlessly when I was round there
for coffee or we were out seine net-fishing. I think that the
scare of Lee's operation had brought him up with a jolt:

152

he felt that he had a whole life still to live and he was not making the most of it.

He pursued all sorts of different possibilities. He thought of going into business but had no capital, thought of other jobs but discovered he lacked the qualifications. Eventually he and Lee decided that the armed forces were the only answer – there would be travel, they would be under the protective umbrella of the Service, accommodation would be found for them, and there would be a new and wider range of people to meet and know. He hoped he might be a pilot. This sounded promising: a dashing extrovert like Joe would be bound to fit in.

There were endless comings and goings after he had made his decision. He applied, had his medicals and what seemed innumerable interviews, and was finally accepted by the Air Force as a potential pilot. As we filled in some of the forms together, in the space where it said 'station of choice' he put boldly in large capitals 'ANYWHERE IN THE WORLD'.

In the evenings, he would get out a map and pinpoint the places in the world where there were still RAF bases that he might get to. Singapore, Aden, Cyprus, Gibraltar, British Guiana – he imagined himself in all and any of these.

There was a round of parties, and one final super goodbye party at the Churches' the night before they left: Joe to report to an RAF station in East Anglia, Lee to move in for the time being with her parents in London.

I was very sad to see them go. They had been good friends, and Pam had looked forward to enjoying Lee's company again after the operation.

I took them to Tadchester station the next day, with piles of cases and boxes, and there was a tearful goodbye from Lee on the station.

'Wherever we go, Bob,' she said, 'we won't have a doctor like you.'

'Send us a postcard from Hong Kong,' I said. 'Best of luck.'

I felt that Joe was doing the right thing. Having become restless, whether it was right or wrong for him to make a move his restlessness would not be satisfied until he had made a change. His choice of the Air Force, what's more, did seem to hold everything he wanted.

Two weeks later I had a phone call from him. He was extremely depressed and down-hearted.

'How are you, Joe?' I asked.

'Awful.'

'You sound close. Where are you?'

'I'm at Winchcombe.'

'That's marvellous,' I said. 'Are you coming for the weekend? I can put you up on the settee in the flat.'

'No,' said Joe. 'You don't understand. I have been *posted* to Winchcombe. Is there any chance of you coming over to see me?'

Poor Joe. He had made this break to get right away from his surroundings – and of all the places had been posted to the Winchcombe RAF Flight Training School.

He sounded so depressed, I shot over to see him that evening. He was sullen and morose.

'Cheer up, Joe,' I said. 'This is a first-class training school and once you have learnt to fly, you may go anywhere.'

'I'm not allowed to fly,' said Joe. 'They found at my final examination I have some high tone deafness and some sinus trouble. I'm not allowed to do any flying.'

'Well, what are you doing?' I said.

'What do you think?' said Joe, 'The only thing I am able to do – they've signed me up as a teacher.'

There were no married quarters available for trainees, so Lee had to stay on with her parents in London. Joe was almost at breaking point. I went to see him several times and each time he was increasingly depressed. He explored all the avenues in the RAF that would take him out of teaching, but nothing seemed to be going right for him.

'I'll see if I can buy myself out and come back to Tad-chester,' he said the last time I saw him. He was being posted away for three weeks to some special drill course which they all had to attend.

When he came back he was a different person. 'I've made it!' he said, triumphantly.

'What? Air crew?' I asked.

'No,' said Joe, 'I've signed up as an RAF parachutist.'

'Rather you than me,' I said.

I lost touch with Joe after that, but some years later I saw him as the leader of the RAF parachutists' team. They were doing a free fall from some incredible height and joining hands in a circle before they opened their chutes and descended.

I wrote to him. From then on I had cards and letters from the places that he had hoped to go, like Cyprus, Singapore, and even one from Saudi Arabia where they had gone to give a free-fall display. He became quite a celebrity and was interviewed on TV.

Good for Joe, I thought. But I never forgot that crest-fallen voice ringing up from Winchcombe.

He had set off bravely to conquer the world and been posted fifteen miles away. I am sure that if he had only asked to be posted to Winchcombe, that would almost have guaranteed that he finished up in Hong Kong.

The only comparable story to that of Joe's was an incident when Frank and Primrose were on holiday in Cornwall. They had been gone about five days when I bumped into them in Tadchester.

'Back already?' I asked.

'Back? Rubbish!' said Frank. 'We spent £3 each on a day's mystery tour – and this is where we have landed up. The place just won't let go of us.'

My patients continued to surprise and entertain me.

One bright-eyed schoolgirl, Penelope Shaw, came into the surgery with a very swollen stomach. She must have been at least six months' pregnant.

She asked for slimming pills to reduce her weight. I insisted on examining her first, and found that she was well and truly pregnant. I questioned her as gently as I could.

'Is there any chance that you could be pregnant?'

'Absolutely none,' said the girl.

I hesitated. 'Have you ever had intercourse?'

'Oh, yes,' she said. 'My boy-friend and I do it every Friday night after Youth Club.'

'Well, don't you think,' I said, 'that this carries a risk of your becoming pregnant?'

'Oh, no,' she said, very positively. 'We had biology lessons at school and I learnt all about having babies before I would let Jimmy anywhere near me. Our biology teacher said you could definitely only become pregnant if you slept with someone. There is no other way, and we have never ever slept together. Jimmy did get a bit dozy once, but I kept him awake. So you see, doctor, there is no chance at all of my being pregnant. I have never ever slept with anyone.'

There was a whole lot of gentle questioning to do. I had to see both sets of parents. The girl was only sixteen, and Jimmy seventeen, but in true Tadchester tradition they got married, had a fine baby, and made a real go of it.

Two years later I saw Penelope pushing a pram. She now had three babies to her name, all fat, healthy children. I guessed that since her marriage she must have started sleeping with Jimmy . . .

I had wondered often about the value of those biology lessons; I expect they are better than nothing at all, but I think the home is the place to learn about the birds and bees. Somehow school seems too detached and dispassionate. It is all a bit of a giggle, and the most inquisitive are often only too eager to do a bit of homework after this particular biology lesson.

In contrast to Penelope was Sandra Reeves, who was about the same age as Penelope. She burst into tears in the surgery as soon as she sat down.

'What is the matter, Sandra?' I said. 'Can you tell me?'

'Oh, doctor,' she said, 'I'm pregnant!'

'Well, how long have you been pregnant?' I asked.

'About six weeks now,' she said.

It did appear, on the surface, that she was better informed then Penelope.

'Did you not use any form of contraceptive?' I asked.

Sandra looked puzzled. 'I am not sure what you mean, doctor.'

'Will you explain to me what happened?'

Sandra, still in tears, stumbled out her pathetic little story.

She had been to a party during a period, and a boy kissed her. This is how she thought babies were conceived – being kissed during a period!

Poor Sandra. I had to give my own sex education lecture to her. I don't think she had slept since the fateful night, and was just about on the edge of a nervous breakdown.

I explained to her, in detail, the process of conception and birth – and it was a very relieved and smiling little girl who left my surgery.

Polly Davies was an unmarried mother, and proud of it. She had a huge, fat, sleepy baby, and I congratulated her on such a fine specimen.

I wondered quite how she managed to cope with a baby as she spent a fair amount of time in and around both The Goat and the Tadchester Arms.

'What do you do with baby when you are out?' I asked.

'Oh, he sleeps all the time. He is never any trouble,' said Polly.

I was a bit worried about her and asked Nurse Plank to pop in some time and just check that all was well.

A couple of days later Nurse Plank turned up at the surgery and showed me a bottle of brown fluid.

'What is that?' I asked.

'*That* is Polly Davies's baby's food.'

'Why is it so brown?' I asked.

Nurse Plank grinned. 'It's quite simple, and no wonder the baby is never any bother. Polly just puts a few spoonfuls of milk powder in half a pint of Guinness and the baby sleeps like a top. I think he is probably the youngest alcoholic in Tadchester.'

One of my favourite patients was Grannie Weedon. She had poor eyesight and lived in a cottage Up-the-Hill.

She had had some constipation trouble. After trying some fairly gentle medicine – which didn't work – I gave her some suppositories which I knew would do the trick.

When I called a few days later there was a disgruntled Grannie Weedon.

'Them things you gave me, doctor, ain't no good at all. You can have 'em back.'

This surprised me. The suppositories I had prescribed were pretty powerful.

'Were they no help at all?' I asked.

'Not a bit,' said Grannie Weedon. 'And they are uncomfortable too.'

I know suppositories are nasty, messy things, but had never heard them described as being uncomfortable.

'You had better let me have a look at them,' I said.

'Here you are,' said Grannie. 'You can take the rotten things away.'

She went to the cupboard and produced a small brown paper bag – full of 3-amp fuses! I could see my suppositories nestling, untouched, at the back of the cupboard. Grannie Weedon's eyesight was obviously not good enough for administering self medication. She was probably one of the few people who could truly say they had blown a fuse!

I had not thought when I saw my patients doing strange things and having strange beliefs that it was I sometimes who could be a source of entertainment and amusement to them.

It was brought home to me when John Denton, the fishing bailiff on the River Tad, came in one morning nursing a finger which looked as if it had been through a mincer. It was obviously very painful, but there was a broad grin on his face.

'What have you been up to now, John?' I asked.

'Just carelessness, Bob. Bloody pike. Makes me feel a right fool.'

John had been catching some big pike which were threatening his stocks of game fish.

'I've had two salmon in the past fortnight with chunks out of their sides,' said John. 'Pike bites. Their eyes are always too big for their bellies, are pikes', and they don't give a bugger what size fish they go for so long as they're lying still.

'Any road, I'd landed this big 'un, and I wanted to treat it gently so that I could hand it over in one piece to the Tadchester Angling Club for one of their lakes. I don't like using a gag* anyway; vicious bloody things they are – do more harm than good.

'So I used friendly persuasion and a few kind words while I was getting the hook out. Bugger me if I didn't pay

* A pike gag is a strong, v-shaped wire spring, with teeth at each end of the 'v', used to hold open a pike's mouth so that the hooks can be taken out without danger to the angler. It's a nuisance, however, can result in a dislocated jaw for the pike, and many anglers prefer to do without it.

attention for a second and the bloody thing had my finger. It spun round as well, while my finger was in its mouth: took the skin off like a Surform file.'

I shuddered as I thought of the lining of a pike's mouth: hundreds of needle-sharp teeth, and all pointing backwards so that anything which got in there had the devil's own job getting out.

But John was smiling again, and every so often, as I cleaned and dressed the finger, would give a suppressed chortle.

'Come on, John,' I said. 'Let me in on the joke. I'm always short of a few laughs at morning surgery.'

'Aye, all right then, lad. Mebbe I shouldn't, but it might be embarrassing for you one of these days. This bloody surgery needs sound-proofing.'

I thought for a second. What medical secrets could have been escaping through the solid walls and thick frosted windows of the surgery door? My God – Charlie Wainwright!

Charlie had been the patient before John. A gnarled Tadchester local, seventy-four years old, and deaf as a post. Like many elderly deaf people, he shouted at the top of his voice during normal conversation. And because he refused to have anything to do with hearing aids – his father and grandfather had never had one and he didn't see why he should break the family tradition at his time of life – anybody talking to him had to shout back.

Charlie had come to see me with a bad attack of constipation.

'I can't go, doctor!' he shouted. 'And I haven't been for nigh on a fortnight. Bloody agony it is. Hard as rock. I want some of that stuff you gave Wagger Martin last Easter. Soon shifted him, it did.'

'Yes, yes, Charlie,' I said. 'The first thing is for me to examine you.'

'Eh? Whatcha say?'

'I HAVE TO EXAMINE YOU. TAKE YOUR TROUSERS OFF!'

Charlie fumbled with his belt, strained at his flies, and then hit a snag.

'YOU'LL HAVE TO TAKE YOUR BOOTS OFF FIRST, CHARLIE! I yelled. '*And* YOUR BICYCLE CLIPS!'.

'Bloody 'ell. All I want is some o' that stuff you gave Wagger Martin. Went straight through him like a dose of . . .'

'YES, YES, CHARLIE. BUT I STILL HAVE TO EXAMINE YOU. JUST LIE DOWN THERE ON YOUR STOMACH WHILE I LOOK AT YOUR BACK PASSAGE.'

Charlie eventually negotiated his boots, bicycle clips, trousers and long johns and lay on the examination couch, still muttering about the stuff I had given Wagger Martin last Easter.

'First the good news, Charlie,' I said. 'Nothing wrong with you there. You haven't got piles.'

'Eh? Haven't got what?'

'PILES!' I screamed. 'YOU HAVEN'T GOT PILES!'

'I know that. I've got constipation. Some o' that stuff you gave . . .'

I got Charlie over on to his back and examined his abdomen. It was, as Charlie had said, as hard as rock.

'YES, CHARLIE. YOU CERTAINLY ARE CONSTIPATED. I'M GOING TO GIVE YOU SOME OF THE STUFF I GAVE WAGGER MARTIN . . .'

I didn't know that the whole shouted conversation was carrying to the waiting-room, and that the patients in there were convulsed with laughter and capping each other's bawdy remarks as poor old Charlie struggled back into his long johns, trousers, boots and, of course, bicycle clips.

Charlie had seemed quite surprised, and a little disappointed, that I gave him a prescription for the laxative instead of handing the bottle to him there and then.

I made three resolutions then. To talk old Charlie into a

hearing aid, to keep my voice down in future – and to
have the surgery sound-proofed.

There was one consolation: I'd never seen, nor have I
seen since, a chirpier lot of patients than those who
followed Charlie that morning ...

CHAPTER 15

On her pre-wedding visits to Tadchester, Pam had become accepted and involved in the Tadchester community. Our flat at Herbert Barlow's was now fully furnished and in apple-pie order. It looked as if it was as anxious for us to occupy it as we were to share it.

Pam had got to know and like my friends and we had been invited out to dozens of dinner and cocktail parties. The time just could not go quickly enough until she was down with me permanently. We had been guests at the de Wyrebock wedding, and Marjorie was now firmly Mrs Charteris.

The night before her wedding her husband-to-be, Paul

Charteris, came to me in great distress. Would I look at his leg?

He slipped off his trousers to show a huge, blistered, inflamed area on the inside of his left thigh and some large, tender glands in his groin. I was puzzled about how it had occurred, and went carefully through his history, looking for clues.

He remembered that his leg had itched one night and he had scratched it. About three days later, this eruption had appeared.

Apart from his worries about getting through the actual wedding ceremony, they were booked on a Kenyan safari for their honeymoon, and he was terribly anxious to be fighting fit for both.

'It's almost as if you had a smallpox vaccination there,' I said.

'Oh, I have been vaccinated recently,' said Paul. 'But that was in my arm.'

The penny dropped.

'Let's have a look,' I said.

Paul took off his jacket and rolled up his sleeve. There was a red, swollen area extending over most of his upper arm. His vaccination had taken with a vengeance.

'It itched like hell,' he said. 'I'm afraid that I did scratch it the odd time or two.'

'What you've done in scratching the vaccination on your arm,' I said, 'is to get some vaccine in your fingernails. When you scratched your thigh you managed to re-vaccinate yourself: this second vaccination has become infected. There's one benefit out of all this, though: you stand no chance whatever of getting smallpox.'

'How long will it take to get better?' asked Paul

'I'll give you some antibiotics and some cream,' I said, 'but I doubt whether it will be completely better before a week or ten days.'

Paul's face fell.

'Whatever you do,' I continued, 'keep it covered and

don't let anything rub against it.'

Paul's face fell even further.

'You are obviously very sensitive to smallpox vaccination. If you're not very careful, you'll have it all over
your body.'

Like the true blue-blooded aristocrat he was, Paul took
the verdict with a stiff upper lip, which meant pulling his
expression back to its normal public school impassivity.

My thoughts flew to his poor wife-to-be, Marjorie. She
had waited so long to get to the starting gate – and now
that she was almost there, she was going to have to spend
at least a further week in the saddling enclosure.

The de Wyrebock wedding was the great social
occasion of the Tadchester year. There was a huge
marquee on the lawn of the de Wyrebocks' house, and
there must have been at least a thousand guests. Caterers
had been brought down from London, and the cost of it
all must have been tremendous. The champagne flowed
freely and the caterers didn't stint the caviare.

Everybody seemed to be called Charles or Angela, that
is when they were not calling each other *Daa-aah-ling*.
Although it was high summer in the grounds of the Big
House, it sounded like lambing time on the farm.

Mrs de Wyrebock was most gracious to me in spite of
the fact that I was one of the few people wearing an
ordinary suit. All the other guests, male guests that is,
were in morning dress. I'd had no choice: I certainly
couldn't afford to hire a morning suit twice and I had
felt my best suit would be up to the occasion. The
impending cost of my own wedding was about to leave me
much less well off than my usual state, which was penniless,
and on top of that we were booked for a honeymoon in
Cornwall. What with the presents for the bridesmaids and
everything, I couldn't see myself getting both ends to
come within shouting distance of each other, let alone
meet.

Paul Charteris conducted himself with great dignity

throughout the ceremony and reception. He must have been in great discomfort as he was towed round by Marjorie to greet each guest, but showed no sign of it, apart from the occasional well-bred wince.

Pam and I hardly knew a soul there, and scarcely anyone spoke to us. We made ourselves inconspicuous behind a hedge in the Italian garden, sat on a bank and ate our lobster salad and drank our champagne.

'This makes our wedding look rather teeny,' said Pam.

'Don't you worry,' I replied, squeezing her hand. 'They've just got quantity here. We have insisted on quality.'

She laughed.

I found that aristorcatic English blue-bloods in their morning coats and grey toppers behaved very much like rugby-playing medical students whenever there was a free bar. Before long our privacy was interrupted by elegantly dressed young men trying to find a place in which to be discreetly and elegantly sick. On our way back to the marquee, we saw a girl of about eighteen or nineteen, straight out of *The Tatler*, in a beautiful white lace dress, absolutely sparko, flat out on the ground behind a laurel bush while her escort tried in vain to revive her by fanning her with his grey topper.

Pam and I paid our respects to Commander and Mrs de Wyrebock and made good our escape.

The party went on all through the night. The following morning a lengthy procession of cars crept its weary way out of Tadchester, the occupants sitting stupefied behind the chauffeurs, trying to remember whether or not they had enjoyed themselves.

Apparently a bunch of the young bloods had gone down into the town for a midnight bathe in the Tad. They stripped to their underpants and splashed across the muddy flats into the water. Two of the girls who followed collected all the young men's clothes and put them in the ladies' public toilet, one of the features of Tadchester Quay.

After the swim there was nothing the young men could do but invade this very private territory. One stout lady holidaymaker, out later than she should have been, had called in to dispense with some of her evening's refreshments before going back to her digs. The sight of six wet young men in clinging underpants invading the Holy of Holies was a little too much for her, and she had to be carried outside and revived by the administration of some very expensive champagne.

During Pam's visits to Tadchester, I had driven her around the surrounding countryside as much as my free time had allowed. The country and coastline were magnificent, and as we went round we looked for a place where we would eventually like to settle. We reckoned that we would have perhaps two or three years in the flat at Herbert Barlow's. Then, hopefully, we would have saved enough money to buy a house.

There were many nice houses, but they were either too expensive or lay right in the path of the holidaymakers who came thundering down to Tadchester in their thousands every year. The summer traffic sometimes got so congested that it could take more than an hour just to cross Tadchester Bridge.

I took Pam to meet Reg Dawkins and his wife, Mary. For me, they were a regular every-other-Tuesday visit. Reg had an obscure disease which kept him confined to a wheelchair. Not a lot, medically, could be done for Reg – my treatment was to call in once a fortnight and share a bottle of his home-made wine.

I usually went there to get myself cheered up. In spite of his disability, Reg was always full of high spirits, had always some outrageous story to tell me. His home-made wine, which was his pride and joy, usually knocked me for six and I had developed a great respect for it. Reg had plenty of time to practise making his special brews and their potency was just something less than neat alcohol. I had warned Pam about their efficacy. After one glass she had learned for herself: she was bright-eyed and sparkling and much more talkative than usual.

'Would your intended like a glass of the dandelion?' asked Reg.

'No,' I said. 'She's got to develop a special stomach lining before she can cope with your stuff. I want to keep her alive at least until our wedding day.'

I changed the subject. 'Reg, if you had to buy a house round here, where would you choose?'

'Altriston, without a doubt,' he said. 'They still live in the Stone Age there, but it's a good village – and it's well away from the holidaymakers.'

'When are you going to take me there?' asked Pam.

'Not until after the wedding,' I replied. 'It's going to take us all our time to get home after Reg's wine.'

'Just one sip of the dandelion for you and your good lady,' said Reg, looking pleadingly at me and already pulling the cork.

'All right,' I said firmly. 'But just one.'

Pam was asleep by the time we got to the Harts', where she was staying. I woke her but she was giggly and drowsy. I had to go round to her side, open the door, put her over my shoulder in a fireman's lift, and carry her upstairs and put her on the bed, where she fell fast asleep again.

'Is Pam all right?' asked Jack Hart as I came down the stairs.

'Oh yes, Jack,' I replied. 'Just a little bit car-sick. Well . . . that, and a drop of Reg Dawkins's wine.'

Jack laughed. He knew the feeling.

It wouldn't be too long now before I no longer had to leave Pam in other people's houses, and then we would keep an eye open for suitable properties in Altriston.

*

The village of Altriston lies five miles inland and directly north-east of Tadchester. It is a compact village with a main street, a surrounding cluster of about fifty cottages, one pub, one post office-cum-store, and a pottery. It is dominated by the Manor House, which stands on some high ground overlooking the village.

Until just before the Second World War it was a feudal village, owned by and under the patronage of the Manor. When Lord Tyster, Lord of the Manor, died in 1937 the estate was split up and the villagers were given the option of buying their cottages.

Lord Tyster had ruled his domain with a rod of iron and laid down strict rules for the village and the villagers. All the cottages had to be painted in the same colours – green and yellow – and be kept in a state of olde worlde picturesqueness. The villagers were forbidden to cut the ivy which covered every cottage. In time the cottages almost disappeared under masses of foliage, which ruined the brickwork, harboured vermin and let in the damp.

During his daily drive through the village – when any villager not touching his forelock would be in danger of instant dismissal – Lord Tyster's evil eye would spot the merest trimming of the ivy, let alone any serious short-back-and-sides treatmeant.

On the night of his death, the villagers gathered at the Manor House to pay their last respects to their master. He died in the early evening: the church gave muffled peals of bells on his behalf, and the flags were flown at half-mast.

Respects paid, the villagers retired to their homes, but not to sleep. Through much of the night there was activity and noise, with torches flashing up and down the main street.

The morning sun broke on to a transformed village. There was not a leaf of ivy to be seen anywhere.

It was not only Lord Tyster who had dominated the village. His only daughter – Rose – had been an absolute tyrant. If a horse had not been groomed to her satisfaction, she would take out her riding crop and thrash the groom there and then. When any youth working on the estate reached his eighteenth birthday, so qualifying for the minimum agricultural wage, he would be sacked on the spot. And it would be Rose Tyster who did it, and took a delight in doing it.

At one time the practice used to have a branch surgery in the village, but it became uneconomical to staff and run and so was closed. Once or twice a month I did a round of visits in the village; anyone else requiring attention would leave a note at one of my regular calls. I would take prescriptions back to Tadchester to have them made up and the next day the carriers would take them to Altriston and leave them at the Post Office Stores where the villagers would pick them up with their shopping.

One of my regular visits was to Jack Wilson, a widower. I used to call once a month and check his blood pressure, then sit down and join him in a pot of tea. He was my local historian and I could – and sometimes did – sit and listen for hours to his tales of bygone days and the history of events in the village. He was a delightful, gentle man, and told his tales without any bitterness or malice.

'He was a great patriot, was Lord Tyster,' said Jack. 'When the First World War broke out, on the very first day he gathered all the estate workers together and ordered them to volunteer for the Army. It were terrible. My wife's late father were over age, and her brother were under age, but they both had to go, and they both got killed.

'There were thirty-three men from this village killed in t'First World War. It were highest rate for size of village in the whole country. There were only three killed in t' Second World War, so it just shows you . . .

'At that time, thank God, I didn't live in Altriston. I worked as a gardener ten miles away. This was my wife's village: I came here when I got married after the First War. I were in the Middle East fighting the Turks. We had a right do there. I left a lot of my mates behind in Mesopotamia. But I reckon I'd have left a lot more behind in France – or maybe stayed there with them – if I'd been with the lads Lord Tyster ordered out to get themselves killed.'

It seemed as if in those bad old days people lived out their lives in a cloud of injustice and ill-treatment. Freedom of choice, alternative employment and housing had been impossible to come by under Lord Tyster. The cutting of the ivy had symbolised a complete change of life-style: people would from then on be free to come and go, to own their own houses and no longer have to touch their forelocks when their lord and master went by.

But the days longed for and talked about most by the villagers were in fact those good old bad old days – when you lived under the protective umbrella of someone who took the ultimate responsibility for you and made the major decisions for you. It was Lord Tyster who paid the bills if anyone had to go to hospital for a prolonged stay; it was Lord Tyster who paid for the education of any village boy or girl who showed exceptional academic promise. People had long ago got used to and accepted this way of life for generations: for good or ill, better or worse, it was their inheritance.

'We were all pleased to see Lord Tyster go because we wanted to manage on us own,' said Jack. 'But we did not realise how difficult it was. We all knew our proper place. I did. So did my Dad and his Dad before him. It's all cars and television and washing machines now, but it'll be a long time before things are proper again.'

I think Jack was right.

For several years the pattern of life in this country did not change much. Suddenly, in a couple of decades between the wars, it was all different. But people were not flexible enough to change at the same speed, and many of the problems of today's society arise from the fact that the changes have been too swift for people to adjust properly.

Altriston had the best of both worlds: all the benefits of a small community without its disadvantages – once Lord Tyster was out of the way, that is. As the older people died, young people took over the cottages, and these tended to be young people from outside.

These new, younger inhabitants benefited by being part of an established rural community. They were able to join in such activities as the Flower Show, the Harvest Festival, the Nativity Play, and other long-standing communal events. As most of them worked away – many commuted to places like Winchcombe – they had interests outside the village which they brought back with them, and which widened the outlook of the community beyond its old insularity. There was a good balance of young and old, and a good community spirit. There were enough willing and fit hands to take care of and keep an eye on the not-so-fit.

The inevitable forces of change had destroyed the old order. (In Lord Tyster's case it was the one change which really is inevitable.) But the same changes which brought the young off-comers to the village in a strange way restored the pattern.

There was never any danger that someone in the village would be left for days unattended. Neighbours were neighbourly, and everyone was called on by at least one other person each day. The old order had given place to the new, but it still worked. And however efficient socialised medicine becomes, it will have a job to match up to the sheer efficiency and humanity of a small community looking after its own.

CHAPTER 16

As the summer wore on, most of my thinking time was taken up by our approaching wedding. I had become so preoccupied that I occasionally wrote the same medication twice on the same prescription. I even wrote my new address in the place where the number of tablets should have been.

The wedding seemed to belong to everybody but Pam and me. There were continual discussions about invitation lists. Did we think that Auntie Enid would make it from Maltby? Could we avoid asking Uncle Jim who always got drunk and embarrassed people? We put down the names of all the possible guests. They came to 320 – and we had set a limit of 120. All the hours of building up the list had to be followed by hours of heart-breaking pruning.

Pam had asked Janice and Zara to be bridesmaids. That is, Janice would be a matron of honour and Zara (who was to marry Eric the month after us) would be a bridesmaid in the true sense of the word.

The artistic, creative Zara insisted that she would design and make the bridesmaids' dresses. Only too pleased to have one less job, we left it to her.

It was all go, and I didn't seem to have a spare minute. On my weekends off I rushed to London to my mother's or to Pam's parents at Leatherhead. When I was on week-end duty, Pam used to come down to Tadchester. I couldn't believe that other weddings were like ours. We had set up an organisation that involved enough planning to rival that of the D-day landing. We had to make decisions about choirboys, organists, church bells, wedding cars, wedding cakes, flowers and a hundred other things.

We had a long plodding interview with the vicar, or to give him his correct title, Prebendary.

Preb. Thomas was really concerned that we were quite familiar with the facts of life. He insisted on telling us in great detail about the birds and bees and was quite unimpressed that I had been involved with the delivery of babies as a student, house doctor and general practitioner for at least six years.

Pam's parents were marvellous. Her father, a tall, ascetic-looking engineer whose main love was horse racing, arranged a reception at the Bull Hotel which would not let him down in the eyes of his friends at the Eccentric Club.

Pam's mother, May, loved all the fuss and was determined to make the most of her only daughter's nuptials. She was a woman of great courage, having had major operations to both hips for osteoarthritis before the days when these operations were completely satisfactory. The operations were designed only to relieve pain and did not give the mobility that present operations do. May somehow overcame all her walking difficulties and wasn't going to miss a trick or be left out of anything. In spite of the great physical discomfort of getting about, she was here, there and everywhere, looking after present lists, dealing with florists, deciding how many relatives she could put up and where to fit in the ones she couldn't.

At the surgery there was a constant stream of well-wishers, and patients leaving presents. Gladys loved it all; you would have thought it was she who was getting married. She was the source of information to the world at large, received the gifts over the counter as if they were for her, and kept meticulous lists of whom I should write to and whom I should go and see. There was more surgery chat about the costume Gladys was going to wear at the wedding – she was to represent the surgery staff – than there was about the bridal gown.

Steve was coming up for a few days to stay with relatives nearby, and Patsy and Henry Johnson were driving there and back in a day, with Jack Hart holding the fort until Henry got back to share the duties I tried to imagine Henry in a top hat: it would make him about ten feet tall.

I had a bachelor night out in Winchcombe with Joe, Frank, Eric and Kevin, which almost ended in disaster. We had drunk almost all the Winchcombe hostelries dry, or that's how it felt, and on the way back I decided we must have some fish and chips to help soak up the beer.

We were on the main trunk road out of Winchcombe, a dual carriageway, with the two lanes separated by a wire fence. The fish and chip shop was on the other side of the road. I got across to the shop without mishap, bought my fish and chips and started to walk back with the newspaper-wrapped bundle which somehow seemed to upset my balance.

As I climbed the wire barrier to cross to the car in the lay-by, there was a sudden rush of wind. I didn't take much notice: I was too busy concentrating on walking steadily with my fragrant burden. When I got to the car I found Kevin, Joe, Frank and Eric white-faced and trembling.

'What's the matter with you lot?' I said. 'Can't you take your drink?'

'Get in, you silly bugger,' said Frank, 'and let's get off the road as quickly as we can. You were bloody nearly killed.'

Apparently when I was walking back, in my cups and concentrating on my fish and chips, I hadn't bothered to check whether there was any traffic. The rush of wind was a Jaguar car belting along at about 90 m.p.h. and which missed me by inches. The riotous evening came to a very subdued end after that.

Some years later I went to the bachelor night of the new junior partner we had appointed, Ron Dickinson. Having consumed a lot of beer at a lot of pubs, Ron appeared at the last pub with two rounds of champagne cocktails. In a few minutes we had all changed from being pleasantly merry to being completely drunk. Going home, Ron had in his car with him his best man, a young vicar friend who was to officiate at the wedding, and Ralph Upton, his father-in-law-to-be.

When they came to a Y-junction in the road, Ron declined the option of both the left and the right and hit the bank in the middle, bursting a tyre.

Nobody was hurt, but Stan, his best man and the young vicar were so full of booze that all they were able to do was to stagger out of the car and lie down on the bank, leaving father-in-law-to-be to change the wheel on his own. I often wondered what Ralph Upton, a local banker, thought as he changed the wheel – looking down at the insensible man to whom he was entrusting his daughter's future life.

I had had to go to Winchcombe to be fitted out with a

top hat and morning coat. Eric, who was going to be my best man, came with me. We both felt ridiculous standing in the mirrored fitting room in our tails, striped trousers and top hats.

'It's good practice for you,' I said to Eric.

'Don't you believe it,' said Eric. 'Zara is insisting on her own sort of white wedding. We are both going to wear some sort of white boiler suit. You know Zara. I haven't seen my outfit yet – I dread to think what it's going to be like.'

I went down to Leatherhead with Eric and Zara and spent my wedding eve at the Bull Hotel where the reception was to be held. My mother was staying there, as well as assorted relatives from both families. Uncle Bertie, my mother's brother, was acting as her escort, and kept us all amused.

Uncle Bertie was a great character who had had an amazing variety of jobs. He had been a dentist's apprentice in the days when dentists were apprenticed, a professional footballer, an electrician, a film studio engineer and manager of a grocery store. He had been a great man-about-town, a ladies' man, and there was a whispered story of his being married and leaving his wife on their wedding day. Although he was obviously never going to be very economically successful, he lived and enjoyed life absolutely to the hilt.

In my student days, when I was reluctantly doing some boxing, Uncle Bertie was one of my greatest supporters. Sporting crowds were the sort of company he loved. Boxing my heart out in some packed East End hall, I would hear his voice boom out from the back 'Come on the blond tiger!' I wasn't blond, and the last thing I could be called was a tiger, but it did distract the crowd from me. They were torn between watching my flailing inexpert arms in the ring and listening to Uncle Bertie's flow of wit from the back of the hall. He could have made a living as a stand-up comic in any company. Thankfully, he had promised to behave himself for the wedding.

I got to bed as early as I could but hardly slept. My mind was in a tremendous turmoil. What did it mean to be married? Was I ready to be? Was Pam ready to be? I eventually drifted off to sleep and woke early to a sunny day, with Eric looking sombrely at me from the door. He had a bottle of whisky in his hand, which he was offering me for breakfast. Eric had already had a couple of snorts. The duties of best man seemed to be worrying him more than mine as groom.

'I've got the ring safely here,' said Eric, patting his lower waistcoat pocket.

'Let's have a look,' I said.

Eric probed in his pocket for a few minutes, getting redder and redder.

'Christ, it's not here!' he said. 'There's a hole in my pocket.'

I put my finger into the lining of his pocket, and it went straight through a large hole. We felt along the front edge of his waistcoat and located the ring at its lowest point. We were able to work it along up through the hole in the lining, back into daylight again. Eric was sweating. I feared the wedding was going to be too much for him. He wasn't cut out for such heavy responsibility, and the early-morning whisky hadn't helped. We found another waistcoat pocket, made sure that it was hole-free, wrapped the ring in tissue paper and put it safely away.

'It's coffee for both of us,' I said to Eric. 'You'll be giving me a nervous breakdown.'

The wedding was to be at noon. At eleven o'clock the Johnsons arrived. Henry did *not* look ten feet tall in his top hat – he looked twelve feet if he looked an inch. Patsy looked as well groomed as ever. They had left Tadchester in the early hours and had driven straight through to Leatherhead. Well, they had *almost* driven straight through to Leatherhead . . .

Henry lived Up-the-Hill in a large house approached by

a long winding drive. Some time back, the local council had refused to come all the way up the drive to collect his dustbins. So, every week since, the dustbins had been put in the back of the estate car, driven to the end of the drive, deposited and left for emptying.

Henry and Patsy had started off for the wedding in the dark and hadn't inspected the car too closely, though Patsy had decorated the bonnet with one or two bows of white ribbon.

Henry was resplendent in a morning suit. Patsy in long pale blue dress with a huge floppy wide-brimmed hat. They were about fifty miles on their way when Patsy complained there was a smell of rotting food.

'Rubbish,' said Henry, 'we must have passed something.'

After a few miles Henry snapped: 'I guess you're right. There *is* a smell somewhere. We'd better go round and have a look.'

He stopped the car, got out, walked round the back, and there, in the space behind the back seat of the estate car, were two dustbins – filled to the top with a week's refuse.

'My God!' said Henry. 'We can't take these to the wedding.'

The ever-resourceful Henry drove on, until they came to a gang working on the road. He got out in his full wedding gear, as if it was the most natural thing in the world, went up to the foreman and asked if he could leave the dustbins with him for a few hours until he returned.

'Don't you worry, guv',' said the foreman, 'we will treat them as if they wuz us own.'

Somehow Henry kept his dignity as the grinning workmen unloaded the bins. He slipped a pound note into the foreman's hand, got into the car and drove on.

By the time Eric and I set out for the church it had begun to drizzle. We walked self-consciously up the aisle, sat in our places, and tried to interpret the noises as the church filled up behind us. Every two minutes Eric checked that the ring was still safely in his pocket. The church was brightly lit, and had been filled with flowers by the tireless May. It looked quite beautiful.

The huge double doors at the back of the church were continually opening and closing, and the murmur of voices increased as the church filled. Just about twelve o'clock, the time I was expecting Pam to arrive, I heard the doors open and shut once again. The murmur of the congregation that had hushed a little at the sound of the doors changed to a concerted gasp. There was a groan from Eric: 'Oh God, whatever will she make me wear at *our* wedding?'

I turned round.

Standing in front of the closed doors were Janice and Zara. They had obviously come in out of the rain to wait for Pam. The bright lights in the church acted as a spotlight on them as they stood framed by the dark oak panels.

Zara's bridesmaids' dresses were exotic creations of some floating gossamer-like material. The fittings must have been done in a very soft light indeed because, with the bright lights of the church and the dark background, the dresses were almost transparent. They were hardly visible at all – and neither girl was wearing a slip. From where I sat it looked as if Janice who, to put it politely, was on the plump side, was just wearing a spotted bikini bra and pants. The curvaceous Zara, who scorned things like bras, looked completely naked except for a brief pair of black pants that would have been banned on any Spanish beach. The bridesmaids smirked rather self-consciously at the impression they had made, having no idea how they made it!

Happily the scene was interrupted by Pam's entrance on her father's arm. She looked absolutely lovely – and, thank God, her long white dress and train were completely opaque.

The wedding ceremony went on as a sea of words and music. I seemed out of touch with the goings-on, and was conscious only of Pam holding my hand as I made my vows. Preb. Thomas was intoning away in a nasal voice and, after what seemed a relatively short time, he placed his hands on our heads. Lifting his voice above even his usual crescendo, he said: 'I now declare you man and wife.'

There was a short prayer, then we stood up and Preb. Thomas began to lead us to the vestry. Eric started to tug at my sleeve.

'Oh God,' I thought. 'He has flipped.'

Eric looked terribly agitated about something. Janice and Zara, seeing his confusion, took an arm each and swept him into the vestry, followed by my mother and Uncle Bertie and Pam's mother and father. The verger had the register open for us to sign and Preb. Thomas was putting everybody at their ease – everybody except Eric who was getting more and more agitated. He kept on trying to interrupt, squeaking, 'Excuse me! Excuse me!'

Eventually the rather irritated Preb. Thomas said, 'What is it, my man?'

'I've still got the ring,' said Eric in a hushed voice.

I was not on the spot when Lot's wife was turned into a pillar of salt, but Preb. Thomas must have given a pretty close imitation. He stood silently for a minute recovering himself. Clearing his throat, he said, 'I must deeply apologise to everyone. I have omitted part of the service. I will have to ask you to return to the church where I will bless the ring.'

We all trooped back into the church. The organ struck up a triumphant march and the congregation stood up, smiling. To everyone's amazement, instead of walking down the aisle we returned to our marriage positions. It was too much for the organist, or the organ, or both. The triumphant march stopped and the organ let out a wail like a deflating bagpipe.

I had not liked Preb. Thomas much so far, but now not only did I warm to him and pity him – I admired him. He left us standing at the steps and went up into the pulpit. There were tears in his eyes.

'Ladies and gentlemen of the congregation, bride and groom,' he said. 'In a lifetime's devotion to the Church I have conducted many hundreds of marriage services. I know the ceremony so well that I no longer use my prayer book during the service. Today, by not taking proper care, I have missed out the ceremony of the blessing of and giving of the ring. I trust that all of you – and God – will forgive me.'

There was a deathly silence in the church as he came down from the pulpit and blessed the ring. I placed it on Pam's finger and we all returned to the vestry. Most of the people there spent the time consoling Preb. Thomas rather than congratulating Pam and me.

Uncle Bertie, who looked as if he had had a few too many before the service, slapped Preb. Thomas on the shoulder and said, 'Cheer up, Vicar, you have given them a wedding that no one will ever forget.' It broke the ice, and we formed up to march down the aisle once more.

The organ, though a bit tentative at first, as if not wanting to be caught out twice, burst into the wedding march. The church bells began to ring. As we walked down the aisle the congregation was just a sea of smiling faces. We moved too quickly for me to put names to them; it all seemed a smiling, laughing blur.

Pam squeezed my hand as we reached the church door. When we got outside the rain had stopped and the sun was shining.

'Hello, husband,' said Pam.

'Hello, wife,' said I, looking into her smiling face.

We hugged.

Life was going to be different from now on.

POSTSCRIPT

There is the fable of the old man sitting outside a town, being approached by a stranger.

'What are they like in this town?' asked the stranger.

'What were they like in your last town?' replied the old man.

'They were delightful people. I was very happy there. They were kind, generous and would always help you in trouble.'

'You will find them very much like that in this town.'

The old man was approached by another stranger.

'What are the people like in this town?' asked the second stranger.

'What were they like in your last town?' replied the old man.

'It was an awful place. They were mean, unkind and nobody would ever help anybody.'

'I am afraid you will find it very much the same here,' said the old man.

If it should be your lot to ever visit Tadchester, this is how you will find us.

A selection of bestsellers from **SPHERE**

FICTION

CHANGES	Danielle Steel	£1.95 ☐
FEVRE DREAM	George R. R. Martin	£2.25 ☐
LADY OF FORTUNE	Graham Masterton	£2.75 ☐
POMEROY	Gordon Williams	£1.95 ☐
FIREFOX DOWN	Craig Thomas	£2.25 ☐

FILM & TV TIE-INS

THE DUNE STORYBOOK	Joan Vinge	£2.50 ☐
SUPERGIRL	Norma Fox Mazer	£1.75 ☐
WHAT DO DOOZERS DO?	Michaela Muntean	£1.50 ☐
MINDER – BACK AGAIN	Anthony Masters	£1.50 ☐
ONCE UPON A TIME IN AMERICA	Lee Hays	£1.75 ☐

NON-FICTION

BACHELOR BOYS – THE YOUNG ONES' BOOK	Rik Mayall, Ben Elton and Lise Mayer	£2.95 ☐
THE BOOK OF SPORTS LISTS	Craig and David Brown	£2.50 ☐
THE HYPOCHONDRIAC'S HANDBOOK	Dr. Lee Schreiner and Dr. George Thomas	£1.50 ☐
WORST MOVIE POSTERS OF ALL TIME	Greg Edwards and Robin Cross	£4.95 ☐
THE FASTEST DIET	Rosie Boycott	£1.25 ☐

All Sphere books are available at your local bookshop or newsagent, or can be ordered direct from the publisher. Just tick the titles you want and fill in the form below.

Name _____

Address _____

_____

Write to Sphere Books, Cash Sales Department, P.O. Box 11, Falmouth, Cornwall TR10 9EN
Please enclose a cheque or postal order to the value of the cover price plus:
UK: 55p for the first book, 22p for the second book and 14p for each additional book ordered to a maximum charge of £1.75.
OVERSEAS: £1.00 for the first book plus 25p per copy for each additional book.
BFPO & EIRE: 55p for the first book, 22p for the second book plus 14p per copy for the next 7 books, thereafter 8p per book.
Sphere Books reserve the right to show new retail prices on covers which may differ from those previously advertised in the text or elsewhere, and to increase postal rates in accordance with the PO.